What other Christian leaders are saying about *Perilous Pursuits*

Joe Stowell has pinpointed the heart of modern man's dilemma— obsession with self. An important book . . .

> *Chuck Colson*
> *Chairman, Prison Fellowship Ministries*

Some people pursue God with stout-hearted allegiance, proudly proclaiming they are "fully committed" to Christ. But after reading *Perilous Pursuits*, I'm reminded that our real pursuit means coming to Him in empty-handed despair. This message will take us all deeper into the heart of God.

> *Joni Eareckson Tada*
> *President, JAF Ministries*

I can't think of a more important topic for our generation . . . Joe Stowell reveals the ugly drive for pleasure, pride and passion in all of us, and gently calls us back to true significance in the person and work of Christ.

> *Bill Hybels*
> *Senior Pastor, Willow Creek Community Church*

Not many books are really important. This one is. A much needed corrective to a dangerous trend in the modern church.

> *Larry Crabb, Jr., Ph.D.*
> *Director, Institute of Biblical Counseling*

In our chaotic "dog eat dog" world, these words are vitally needed. This book should have wide distribution.

> *Adrian Rogers*
> *Pastor, Bellevue Baptist Church*

PERILOUS PURSUITS

JOSEPH M. STOWELL

MOODY PRESS

CHICAGO

ISBN 0-8024-7842-5

1 3 5 7 9 10 8 6 4 2

Printed in the United States of America

This book is gratefully dedicated
to the glory of God
and the
gain of His Kingdom

Soli Deo Gloria

I eagerly expect and hope that
I will in no way be ashamed,
but will have sufficient courage so that now
as always Christ will be exalted in my body . . .

Do nothing out of selfish ambition or vain conceit, but in humility consider others better than yourselves. . . .

Your attitude should be the same as that of Christ Jesus: Who, being in very nature God, did not consider equality with God something to be grasped, but made himself nothing, taking the very nature of a servant, being made in human likeness. And being found in appearance as a man, he humbled himself and became obedient to death—even death on a cross!

Therefore God exalted him to the highest place and gave him the name that is above every name . . .

Philippians 1:20; 2:3, 5–9

CONTENTS

WITH GRATITUDE

Before we start, a word about some people whose love and labor for Christ have proven to be of great significance. Without them this work would not have been possible.

Special thanks go to Martie, my wife, whose insightful responses to this manuscript have been sensitive, objective, and invaluable. So much of who I am is because of her influence in my life. After twenty-seven years, she continues to intrigue and bless me.

I owe a great debt to the editors who have helped on this project: Jim Vincent, whose technical expertise and precision have helped to hone this instrument for its use in the hands of God, and Phil Rawley, who came alongside with good input on organizational matters and illustrative material. Thanks too to Cheryl Dunlop, who came in at the tail end to pinch hit for Jim, who with his wife, Lori, were busy with the arrival of their first child, Jonathan.

I am indebted as well to Susan Robertson, whose time in researching material for this book was done with a marvelous spirit and effective results.

Toward the end of the process we asked several individuals whom we respect to read the manuscript and give us objective feedback. Jim Bell, Susan Robertson, Andy Scheer, Dennis Shere, and Billie Sue Thompson offered helpful advice and perspective. As a result, ministry potential of this book will, by God's grace, be greatly expanded.

During this long and challenging process several have helped with the typing responsibilities. My former secretary, Betty McIntyre, and my current secretary, Lori Imhof, devoted many valuable hours in preparing the manuscript. Beth Longjohn and Andrea Miller have also logged many hours getting this material to the place where it could be legible to the editors.

It wouldn't be right if I didn't take a moment as well to thank the outstanding staff at Moody Press. From Greg Thornton who leads the work of Moody Press, to Bill Thrasher and Jim Bell whose encouragement and suggestions proved to be helpful, to the typesetters, those who get it to press for printing, and our capable people at the distribution warehouse who help to get it into your hands. This project is a combined effort of the Moody Press family.

Most importantly, I owe everything to the Lord, whose truth is my reason for preaching and writing, whose gifts are my enablement, and whose name is worthy of my service to Him.

Without Him all our efforts would be, in the final analysis, insignificant.

PART ONE
REGRET

CHAPTER ONE
THE PURSUIT

The Westminster Shorter Catechism is correct when it concludes that "man's chief end is to glorify God and enjoy Him forever." Why, then, are we so consumed with glorifying ourselves and seeking enjoyment in and for ourselves apart from Him? Perhaps this is the reason we often find life so disappointing, disruptive, and ultimately, full of regret.

W e are built for significance. Our problem is not that we search for it, but that we search for it in all the wrong places.

Barbara, a college sophomore who began her summer with great expectations, landed a good job in a nearby nursing home. But her summer turned into a nightmare. Before it ended Barbara was sexually assaulted by two men on the job. Deciding to drop charges due to the complicated and embarrassing legal process, Barbara found support and strength from her parents and church family.

In particular, three young men in the church sought her out to encourage and help her through the trauma. Each asked her out for an evening of fun to get away from it all. But before the evenings were over, each had asked her for sexual favors.

Struggling with a sense of deep disappointment and confusion, Barbara felt that her worth and value had been trampled. Why, she wondered, did men seem so free to use and abuse her, seeing her only as an object of their gratification? The answer came, and her liberation began, in her next semester at college as Barbara realized that she was being driven by a desire to find her sense of significance in having attention from men.

If men were attracted to and interested in her, she sensed her worth. She felt like she counted for something. Her obsession with significance had caused Barbara to order her whole life, from the clothes she wore to what she said and did, around one goal: to gain the attention of men through her sexuality. She never wanted to be provocative and did not try intentionally to be seductive. But in her dress and her words she sent all the wrong signals. Men thought she wanted sex when she was really seeking personal significance.

The irony is that these relationships with men always "went south" for Barbara, finding their way to the dead-end streets of shame, loss, and confusion. No wonder despair had anchored itself in her soul.

But after years of carrying the weight of guilt and seeking deliverance from her struggle through repeated prayer and confession, Barbara found liberation in a fundamental truth: significance is secured not through our efforts or by the attention and affirmation of others; rather her significance *had already been established* in the completed work of Christ for her on the cross. Armed with that reality, Barbara was set free from a life of mixed messages and the ensuing hassles. She began to enjoy meaningful and constructive relationships with the men in her life.

THE SEARCH FOR SIGNIFICANCE

For Barbara, the search for significance had taken a radical turn. Though many of us will not plunge to such depths of difficulty, our search for significance will become debilitating in other arenas of life.

I recall being with a friend of mine, an effective teacher of God's Word, who had just returned from a week of ministry at a national conference in Canada. He was telling me how wonderful it had been to be the teacher in the Bible Hour every morning. He was obviously captured by the privilege and also thrilled with the attendees' enthusiastic response to the teaching of the Word. What he didn't know was that the year before I had been the Bible Hour teacher at that same conference. I had enjoyed the same sense of privilege he was basking in.

Do you think I could be content to encourage him and rejoice with him? I'm embarrassed to say no. I kept waiting for him to take a breath, to reach a paragraph break so that I could jump in and tell him that I knew exactly how he felt. And sure enough, at the first verbal pause I was into the conversation, building a monument to me. But I walked away from that conversation asking myself *Why do I feel so compelled to magnify me?*

I felt a loss of dignity and a sense of shame—and that surprised me. I had sought to strengthen and elevate myself; instead, I felt weak and small. I had assumed that if I could enhance myself, I would feel better about myself.

More recently, I was sitting on the platform before 1,200 pastors on the opening night of a recent Pastors Conference at Moody Bible Institute. The keynote speaker began his talk by saying, "When Tim asked me to come and speak at this year's conference. . . ." Immediately I thought about his statement. Tim is my associate, and we work hard to get the finest speakers possible; often we're able to bring in high-profile Christian leaders.

I'm sorry to admit, though, that for a fleeting moment a thought resided in my mind and heart that I wish had never come: *Wait a minute. Tim didn't ask him, I did. I wonder if these pastors know that I am the one who chooses the speakers for this conference.* Thankfully, the thought didn't stay long before it was chased off by a more rational one: *What difference does it really make who chooses the speakers?* Yet that fleeting moment showed me how deeply entrenched this issue of significance is, and how readily we view most of the moments of our lives through its distorted lens.

None of us is exempt from this significance pursuit, to the point where the pursuit often becomes a significance obsession. Our problem is that we look for significance in all the wrong places. We pursue prosperity, power, position, belonging, identity, and affirmation in hopes of finally securing a sense of value and worth.

To make matters worse, this pursuit is complicated by three basic drives: pleasure, pride, and passion. Though not wrong in themselves —they are, after all, given by God—pleasure, pride, and passion turned inward in a search for significance in our own achievements and the commendation of others put us at great peril.

Unless we find our significance in God and His Son, Jesus Christ, we will experience measures of regret instead of the contentment and security that God intends for us.

A pastor's wife who had served with her husband for years came to me after a recent service with tear-filled eyes, saying that she had never realized before how her obsession with significance had created such a bitter and angry spirit toward the people she and her husband served. They did their best to serve the congregation's needs, often denying themselves evenings at home, a social life, leisure, even sleep. For the most part, however, their efforts went unrecognized.

In fact, as is true in all public service, they got mostly criticism and complaints. This woman had counted on finding her sense of significance through her and her husband's efforts, and the congregation's grateful and well-deserved applause. Feeling unloved and unappreciated, her sense of significance trampled, she found anger and bitterness poisoning her heart toward the ministry God had called them to. She was disappointed, her part in the ministry disrupted, and her heart disengaged from God and the people.

But the tears in her eyes were tears of repentance and liberation as she came to realize that the congregation was not the source of her significance. "You're right, I am complete in Christ. His affirmation for faithfulness and effective service is the only thing that really matters. He's the true source of value and worth." This discovery transformed the focus of her life, leaving her free to love and serve regardless of the people's response.

A PRIMAL NEED

All of us are driven by the compelling need to believe that we are significant. I have yet to meet the person who says, "Significance? I couldn't care less. All I want to do is fill space on this planet." Everyone wants to count for something. As author and theologian R. C. Sproul says, "We yearn to believe that in some way we are important. This inner drive is as intense as our need for water and oxygen."[1]

In fact, because our need for significance is so primary, it can easily become an obsession. Modern counseling and psychology have focused a lot of attention on obsessive behaviors, whether it's an obsession with food, tobacco, alcohol, pornography, drugs, power, work—or even an obsession with being abused! But I don't know that I've ever seen a list of obsessive behaviors that includes an addiction to the maintenance, advancement, enlargement, and protection of our significance. Yet for many of us, that is our less-than-magnificent obsession. Just as obsession with food leads to gluttony and an obsession with safety leads to anxiety and even neuroses, an obsession with our significance leads to a life of selfishness.

In psychologist Abraham Maslow's classic study of fundamental human needs, only food and safety rank as more compelling drives than significance. These intrinsic needs manage and manipulate who we are and what we do. Just as hunger drives us to find and consume food to survive, and just as we instinctively defend ourselves when we feel threatened, so we are driven as well to discover, establish, maintain, protect, and enhance our sense of significance.

Feeling significant comes as we believe we have worth, value, and dignity. Significance is knowing that our existence has made a difference after all. It doesn't have to be a great difference, just a difference. Significance is what makes a pat on the back so important. It's why affirmation is so vital. We believe we count when someone says we count. Having value and dignity are important, but depending how we seek them, we can be deluded and consumed by the search. Without a tried and proven strategy, our search for significance is a risky and treacherous adventure.

The search is risky because we live in a world full of other significance seekers who either carelessly or purposely are willing to damage our sense of worth to establish theirs. These people are often fierce competitors who get their significance through the exercise of power and control, who attempt to build the illusion that they are so significant that others will submit to their pleasure and agenda.

These significance seekers attempt to overpower us personally, relationally, sexually, socially, and athletically, and in the process they may very well destroy our sense of worth. Complicating the scene are those of us who find our sense of significance in the attention of these power brokers and as a result become their easy prey. *There is not a realm of life that isn't damaged, sometimes fatally and irretrievably, by the significance seekers of the worlds in which we live.*

REALMS OF REGRET

Yet the problem does not really begin with others pursuing *their* significance at our peril. It begins with the self-inflicted damage we cause in our own significance pursuit. Our obsession with our own significance is such an insatiable hunger that its impact is felt in every area of life, inevitably creating realms of regret that put our sense of worth in peril.

OUR PERSONHOOD

The debilitating effects of our addiction to the enlargement, protection, and maintenance of our significance always strike at our personhood.

This striving to advance our own significance shows up typically when we're driving in traffic. Getting cut off, not being allowed to merge into a lane, or worse yet, getting ticketed for an offense, are all affronts to our sense of significance. As Christians, we may not have enough words and gestures to express how we really feel at moments like that, so we resort to intense stares, muttering under our breath in the hope that the other driver can read lips.

Or we aggressively retaliate. I have had more than one "out of body" experience on the highway after I blew an anger fuse. Hovering over myself I watched in amazement: "Was that really you, Stowell? I had no idea you were like that." Immediately I feel a sense of loss and shame after exalting and defending myself on the interstate.

This obsession with significance is why we are so defensive when someone seeks to improve us through criticism. You'd think we would thank those whom God sends to help knock off our rough edges, but instead we resist their input and intimidate our advisors to protect our sense of significance that has been threatened by criticism.

This obsession is also why some of us are embittered by unchangeable personal realities like our size, shape, color of skin, or physical deformity. Society establishes acceptable norms for our looks and style. When for His good purposes God creates in us some deviation from society's norms, it is easy for us to feel less than significant and culturally unacceptable. This leads to an insecure spirit that damages our capacity to find fulfillment and satisfaction in God's purposes for us.

Similarly, men and women who are disappointed in courtship and remain single can be vulnerable. They may be left with a deep sense of rejection and a haunting feeling of insignificance that makes it hard for them to have any positive relationships with members of the opposite sex.

Our compulsion for significance makes us vulnerable to a legion of verbal sins, including gossip, slander, boasting, lying, immoral chatter, and other unkind blows by our tongues. In all this our character, our personhood, is eroded. The significance addiction leaves us vulnerable to a host of other personal failures that complicate life and debilitate us spiritually and socially. It may surprise you to learn that many people have affairs not because they are drooling with uncontrolled passion, but because for the first time in their lives someone has come along and made them feel significant during a time when they especially needed it.

We are quick to violate basic principles of stewardship and burden ourselves with debt to accumulate things that enhance our significance on the social scene. And to advance our significance in the marketplace, we may violate our integrity as we exchange conscience and commitment to Christ for a significant title on our business card.

Significance seekers are *unable to serve others* unless there is an advantage to be gained, *unable to sacrifice* to advance a cause that is not their own, *unwilling to suffer* if necessary for another's sake, and *unable to surrender to any agenda*—corporate, family, or church—that impedes the progress of their pursuit of significance. This obsession renders us useless in terms of making constructive contributions to our families, friends, society, and churches. And even when managed to magnificent outward success, the significance obsession ultimately brings loss, shame, guilt, emptiness, and regret.

OUR RELATIONSHIPS

Because our personhood affects every relationship we have, few obsessions are more devastating than seeking to satisfy this primal need at the expense of others. Families are victimized by husbands and fathers whose significance is established only when they are in absolute, unchallenged control. Crossing a significance seeker who is the head of the home—a father or single parent—can lead to anger, violence, and other forms of intimidation and manipulation. Significance seekers who head homes like this never say they are wrong or sorry.

We fathers too often are willing to absent ourselves from home as we seek to establish our significance in a place where we feel more capable of accomplishment—the office or even the golf course. We look for compliments and job advancement not to provide for our families but to feed our egos.

Meanwhile, mothers may feel that because motherhood is an undervalued profession they are less significant than they want to be. Sometimes a mother or father, in the name of finding significance, locates a "significant other" and quits the marriage emotionally and then physically, leaving children and spouse to fend for themselves. At other times, workaholic parents neglect time with children, supposing that significance is found in performance. Some parents communicate that a child's significance is measured not in his parents' unconditional love and acceptance, but rather in performing up to their expectations. In these and other ways our misunderstanding of true significance places our families at risk.

Similarly, our significance search affects our friendships. Often we forge friendships simply because we draw significance from associating with the other person. But this only leads to an over-possessiveness and unwarranted jealousy on the part of the significance seeker, which in turn leads to friction and the death of the friendship. Many couples violate basic moral principles in their courtship for fear of losing this person who offers so much significance now and the prospect of future significance in marriage.

Interestingly, our students who work with gangs here in Chicago attest to the fact that very few if any young people join gangs for violence, sex, drugs, and crime. They join because the gang is the only place where they find acceptance and personal significance.

This addiction to significance helps explain why our kids choose friends we don't approve of, and why a well-educated, decent girl gets hooked up with a guy who has nothing to offer but trouble and hurt. That's just the point. He needs her, and that makes her feel significant, accepted, and affirmed. This addiction is why we refuse to forgive and even seek revenge against those who have hurt us.

OUR CULTURE

Not only does a significance addict damage his personhood, bringing loss and regret to himself and his relationships, but many of society's problems reflect the same pattern. Some cultural structures enhance the significance of one race or gender or class over another. Those caught in the lower levels of the system feel a loss of significance, while those in power don't wish to share their significance with others. Thus people march, riot, and even start wars. The poor, the disabled, and the immigrants who feel they are ignored rise up to demand their place and their worth. Some politicians, seemingly caring for others' needs, stand with the underclass with a desire only to inflate their own significance rather than to benefit those they stand with. Homosexuals, people of color, the poor, and women take to the streets to demand a significant place in society.

Such highly dangerous pursuits as rape, abuse, violence, drugs, and crime often are the sad outcomes of a desperate search for significance in a dramatically depersonalized society. Even abortion is an outcome of the search for significance. If an unborn child threatens a mother's agenda for significance, society argues that the child is expendable.

Much of the despair and regret in the world around us can be attributed to our inability to understand and remedy this obsession for significance at any cost. And instead of helping us, society's power structures relentlessly fan the flame.

The constant refrain we hear is that those who are perceived as significant have arrived and are models of the ultimate pursuit of life. In our culture, significance is measured less by the contributions we make to society than by our power, performance, position, and prosperity.

Look at the world of college and professional sports. The message is clear: winners are the only ones who count. There's little applause for finishing second. Character doesn't win pennants. As the late baseball manager Leo Durocher once said, "Nice guys finish last."

Even more debilitating, our society cares little about the integrity or character of significant people or how they became significant. The point is to attain and maintain your significance. The process is irrelevant. Television talk shows specialize in staging and interviewing America's "significant" ones. I'm still waiting for David Letterman or Jay Leno to say, "Now I know you're significant, but what we all want to know is whether you have maintained personal integrity as you've achieved your significance." Madonna would have a hard time fielding that question.

In a sense, ours is a "Little Jack Horner" world where the game of significance ignores the deeper issues of right and wrong. In a moment of what for him was stellar significance, Jack stuck his thumb into a Christmas pie, pulled out a plum, raised it high in the air, and proclaimed, "What a good boy am I." Pleased with his performance, he went public and sought significance through the applause and affirmation of those around him.

But don't forget where Little Jack Horner was sitting. If I remember correctly, "Little Jack Horner sat in a corner." As far as I know, the only reason little boys sit in corners is because they haven't been good. I also know of few mothers who reward their little boys for not being good by giving them a whole pie. It's possible he stole the pie from the kitchen.

However Jack got that pie, what's he doing taking credit for pulling out a plum, since it was his mother who put the plums there? Fundamental decency would require that he give credit to whom credit is due and not heap it upon himself. And even if you don't buy my analysis of the story, we would all have to agree that Jack is in clear violation of acceptable table manners by having his fingers in his food. But there he sits, inviting the applause of the world with what really seems a hollow and silly conquest.

It's this Little Jack Horner syndrome that makes us willing to do whatever is necessary to become significant. But if we ignore the process, we unwittingly erode our sense of worth by clouding our conscience. Regardless of the pinnacle we reach, our significance conquest finally becomes hollow and filled with regrets.

Who on his deathbed doesn't regret not spending more time with his family, or the loss of valued friends he has brutalized in the process of climbing that mount called Significance? Who at the end of it all wouldn't want to reclaim a good name and an upstanding reputation? Who wouldn't trade all the significance of this world for a place in the world to come? "What good is it for a man to gain the whole world, yet forfeit his soul? Or what can a man give in exchange for his soul?" Jesus asks us (Mark 8:36–37).

Christ once described a significantly prosperous, powerful, and well-positioned man who had so much that he built new barns to hold it all. This highly significant person smugly said to himself, "Eat, drink and be merry." Jesus said God's reply to the man was, "You fool! This very night your life will be demanded from you. Then who will get what you have prepared for yourself" (Luke 12:19–20)? His is the ultimate regret, the regret of eternal loss.

THE CAUSE OF CHRIST

Most important, however, our obsession with significance creates another realm of regret that strikes destructive blows to the cause of Christ. Bringing our uncured addiction into the church damages the reputation of Christ, the enhancement of His glory, and the advance of His cause.

There are pastors who use the church as a platform to launch a personal significance campaign. They do battle with deacons, elders, and charter members who also want to use the church to enhance their power and position. The division and disruption that come as a result of these battles stain the reputation of Christ in the community. Added to this is the competition between churches to be the biggest and the best, discouraging faithful smaller works and swelling with pride those who are blessed with more.

There are also those who proclaim that you can satisfy your longing for significance not in Christ and Him alone, but by coercing Him through "faith" to make you happy, healthy, and prosperous. There are televangelists who have preyed on the uninformed by appealing to their need for significance, making these people feel significant if they send money, which in turn enhances the significance of the charlatan preacher.

Still others have dishonored the name of Christ by allowing their significance in His work to delude them into believing that they were above obedience when it came to money, women, or power. They have publicly taken the name of Christ through the trough of disgrace.

THE AUTHENTIC CHRISTIAN

This obsessive pursuit obstructs authentic Christian living. Our obsession with significance stimulates things that are counter to the values and behavior of those who follow Christ. Authentic Christianity does not call for defensive responses, but a vulnerable spirit that we might be taught by the Spirit. Jesus calls us to have a meek and humble heart, like Him (Matthew 11:29).

True Christianity calls us to complement one another, not to compete. It holds us accountable to be people of unflinching integrity and to care more about the kingdom of God and eternity than about material things, regardless of how significant they may make us feel here.

A proper understanding of our walk with Christ plants our security firmly on our unshakable relationship with Him. It speaks against connecting our security to persons or possessions, which only exposes us to the fear of rejection and loss. Christians are not to live to please others or their culture, but rather to please God. The jealousy, greed, possessiveness, and manipulative behavior that characterize significance seekers are inconsistent with faith in Christ. Authentic Christians continue to do well regardless of whether they are recognized or affirmed.

As those who imitate Christ, we don't focus on our rights and privileges, but are willing to sacrifice them for greater gain in His work. We are shaken, but not fatally so, even by significant loss, because we can't lose that which is ultimately significant to us. Gossip, slander, and bragging become unnecessary for those who are growing in Christ. We are to focus on encouraging, helping, and affirming others.

Christ calls us to rejoice with those who rejoice, which frees us to feel good about those who accomplish great things instead of feeling jealous and seeking to bring others down. Following Christ means that we are in control of our priorities and reject the impulse to be either workaholics or leisureholics when it comes to life's important responsibilities.

What is the underlying reason we as Christians often feel a sense of failure as we attempt to accomplish those things we know God wants us to do? The answer may be found at the feet of our addiction to the enlargement, advancement, and defense of our own significance.

IMPACT ON THE CHURCH

The debilitating effects of the Christian's self-centered quest for significance goes beyond the personal to the church at large. Even a casual analysis of American culture reveals that over the last few decades we have turned a dramatic corner. Americans are no longer culturally committed to the Judeo-Christian principles that have undergirded our law and society from the beginning. Americans have now moved into a neo-pagan environment where the values that Christians hold to be nonnegotiable are no longer politically correct. In fact, they are culturally unacceptable.

In a very real sense, we Christians are becoming more and more of an underclass in this society. Our convictions are at best discounted and at worst mocked by the prevalent philosophies promoted by the media and other significant influences. We are increasingly viewed as less-significant people in our culture.

Think what this means if we are obsessed with significance in the eyes of our pagan culture. Our seeking after cultural standing could very well undermine the strength of our faith, and weaken our commitment to stand with courage in the face of subtle opposition and perhaps even open persecution. The history of the church is littered with individual Christians and institutions that sought to remain culturally significant and in the process eroded their commitment and distinctiveness in Christ.

Maintaining a thoughtful, balanced, and just posture within a pagan culture is a worthy goal. But there comes a time when standing for that which is true may invite rejection by a culture whose values are so dramatically opposed to the values of God's kingdom. Our Lord warned clearly in John 15:18–19 that if this world rejected Him, we as followers probably will suffer the same fate.

If we are driven by our need for significance, we will capitulate to the culture to remain in its good graces and lose our ability to make a noticeable difference in our world.

We must keep in mind that the early church advanced the cause of Christ in a culture that viewed Christians not just as irrelevant, but as enemies of the empire. If you named the name of Christ in that day, you lost your cultural significance. You could also wind up as lunch for the lions in the Roman arenas as the crowds roared with excitement.

The early church didn't seek its significance in acceptance and affirmation by the pagan world. It had found its significance in Christ. Their liberation from this obsession gave these believers the capacity to be courageous. As a result, they glorified the significance of His name and advanced His cause in such a compelling way that Christianity ultimately became the official Roman state religion some three hundred years after the death of Christ.

We make a difference when our uniqueness is clothed in the grace and truth of Jesus Christ, not when we capitulate in order to become credible in a pagan society. Great schools have become thoroughly secularized because the faculty and administration desired to be credible and significant in the educational world at the expense of truth, heritage, and their mission. Entire denominations, great movements, churches, and causes throughout history have been derailed because the urge for cultural significance led to compromise in their methods and their message. Their quest for society's approval had more force than truth and a solid commitment to be significant in God's eyes at any cost.

OUR REDEMPTIVE PURPOSE

The greatest danger of our obsession with significance, however, is measured in its crippling effect on our ability to fulfill God's purpose for us—to display His glory to others. Even if our significance obsession would not threaten our personhood, family relationships, authentic Christianity or even an impact on society at large, this peril alone warrants our concern. Scripture affirms that redemption was accomplished in us for the express purpose of releasing us to enhance His glory and advance His cause. (See 1 Corinthians 6:19–20 and Ephesians 1:6, 11–14.)

God's glory through us is the visible expression of His marvelous character in our lives. We display God's glory by replicating all that He is. In the process, we declare His significance and worth by giving Him credit for all that we are and all that we do. In Philippians 1:20 Paul declared: "I eagerly expect and hope that I will in no way be ashamed, but will have sufficient courage so that now as always Christ will be exalted in my body, whether by life or by death" (NASB*).

If we are obsessed with exalting our own significance, we are unable to exalt His significance. The two are mutually exclusive endeavors. You can't have it both ways. Paul said in the next verse "For to me, to live is Christ and to die is gain." If our formula is "For me to live is personal gain and to die is Christ," then we forfeit the essential element of what it means to glorify Christ and His Kingdom.

And if we spend our lives seeking to enhance our significance by acquiring position, power, prosperity, and other cultural status symbols, we disable our capacity for deeds that advance and enhance the kingdom of Christ. To disciples who were worried about this kind of significance, Christ admonished, "Seek first his kingdom . . . ." Until we are liberated from this obsession, we will not be free to glorify God

*New American Standard Bible.

by expressing His significance and doing significant things for His eternal kingdom. And those two objectives are God's primary reason for redeeming and placing us on this planet.

Michelangelo is said to have often painted with a brush in one hand and a shielded candle in the other to prevent his shadow from covering the masterpiece he was creating. As God works through us to craft His glory and gain, we must be careful that our shadows are not cast across the canvas of His work. Being obsessed with our own significance will inevitably shade and distort the project.

THE TRUE SOURCE OF SIGNIFICANCE

Christ and Christ alone is preeminent. He needs no competition. He is the only truly significant Person in the universe. He deserves our commitment to reflect His significance, not our own. In Colossians 1:13–18 Paul cataloged the ultimate, unsurpassed significance of Christ:

> For [God] has rescued us from the dominion of darkness and brought us into the kingdom of the Son he loves, in whom we have redemption, the forgiveness of sins. He is the image of the invisible God, the firstborn over all creation. For by him all things were created: things in heaven and on earth, visible and invisible, whether thrones or powers or rulers or authorities; all things were created by him and for him. He is before all things, and in him all things hold together. And he is the head of the body, the church; he is the beginning and the firstborn from among the dead.

Paul concluded with this affirmation: "So that in everything he might have supremacy."

We cannot express the supreme significance of Christ when we are striving, struggling, and scheming to establish our own. Nor can we "seek first his kingdom" when we are compulsively committed to schemes that advance our the significance of our kingdoms.

How very unusual that John the Baptist, the acclaimed, devout prophet, declared when he saw Christ, "He must increase, but I must decrease" (John 3:30; NASB). How very instructive.

It is safe to say that there is not an area of life that is unaffected by this primal need for significance. But apart from Christ, the passages through which we normally move to establish and maintain our significance, even when successfully negotiated, most often leave us with a sense of sorrow, loss, and regret.

Our need for significance is not the culprit. We were built for significance. The culprit is our struggling, stumbling attempts to manufacture our own sense of significance and in the process place at risk that very thing for which we strive, the very people we need and love, the society in which we move, and the cause of Christ for which we have been redeemed.

CHAPTER TWO
PLEASURE, PRIDE, AND PASSION

> *If it were only a hunger for significance, we might be able to at least hold this craving at bay by a good dose of discipline and a depth of resolve. But to complicate matters, the significance addiction is aided and abetted by a phenomenally powerful trio of surging inner energies called pleasure, pride, and passion. This trio moves within each of us, creating partnerships of power that can corrupt and devastate even the best of us. If left in their pre-redemptive flow, these forces render us incapable of advancing the significance of Christ and His kingdom.*

Richard blew past my secretary and burst into my office with an intensity in his eyes and voice that said he meant business. He demanded that I give him the note his wife had discovered in his drawer—the one he received from their high school babysitter with whom he was having an affair, detailing the pleasures of a recent night at a nearby hotel. As I reached for the note I said, "Richard, I'd like to help if you'll let me." No response. He grabbed it, and slammed the door behind him. Though he had been a part of our church for years, it was the last time I saw him.

For Richard it was clear. Life would be more significant with another woman, without his wife and daughters, without his church and friends. *I feel significant being noticed and wanted by someone young and exciting*, he told himself. *What a pump for my pride and a ready-made outlet for passion and pleasure.* Driven by his primal need for significance, Richard had yielded to the surging power brokers of passion, pride, and pleasure in his soul.

Though Richard tried to ride this tidal wave to satisfaction, his actions propelled him toward insignificance and loss. Pleasure, pride, and passion, the resident manipulators of our inner selves, propel us to seek self-fulfillment. But like Richard, we face a host of tragic consequences as the tidal wave washes over family, friends, and the testimony of Christ. Richard's choices have devastated the lives of his wife, daughters, his high school lover, and himself, with implications for generations to come.

Those restless, inner energies of pleasure, pride, and passion become the perilous impulses for many of us as we seek after our own significance. Indeed, they can become the most volatile realities of our lives. What they do in the depths of our being can clutter and corrupt our whole world.

THE ISSUE OF CONTROL

Before we assume that we are victims of these forces, let's remember that the issue is not their existence but their management. We call the shots regarding where our pleasure, pride, and passion take us. Richard did not have to manage his life from the bunker of his soul the way he did.

IN CONTROL

External forces constantly appeal to our inner energies of pleasure, pride, and passion. A California pastor I know was riding the elevator to his hotel room one evening. The two young and appealing women who were also on the elevator smiled at him and said, "How about some fun tonight?" Who would know? But he looked away and when the door opened, he walked away.

Alone. Tough choice to make. But this minister took action by walking away. Obviously he had a management system within that helped keep those three forces in check.

A leader of a major ministry told me of noticing a lady across the lobby as he checked into a hotel. He reached his room and was loosening his tie when he heard a knock and opened the door. It was her, wanting to come in. For a flash of a moment he paused . . . then closed the door and walked back into the room alone. In that pause he had organized the forces of his heart with productive and peaceful results.

Think of the amazing story of Joseph, working around and with Potiphar's wife (who no doubt was a "pick of the land" given Potiphar's status in Egypt). Day after day, Joseph resisted her seductive advances. Finally, when this woman was at her boldest, he ran from her (Genesis 39:1–12). Joseph demonstrated an unusual command of the inner forces of pleasure, pride, and passion.

His story is duplicated in the lives of thousands of people whose inner management protects them from becoming victims of these volatile forces that can lead them to fractured lives. For every headline marking a failure in the arenas of morality, integrity, public trust, and character, there are myriads of unheralded, faithful people who pause to organize the energies within that empower them to make choices that yield quality outcomes.

OUT OF CONTROL

Periodically, however, the headlines graphically describe how far the mismanagement of our inner forces can take us. Milwaukee's Jeffrey Dahmer ended up where few of us believed a man could go: murder and cannibalism. Dahmer's search for significance somehow got short-circuited as his life veered off into bizarre and brutal expressions of passion, pride, and pleasure.

He is now serving a life term in a Wisconsin prison for killing and mutilating seventeen young men. A strange mixture of forces boiled in the cauldron of his heart and mind. Whether anyone will ever know how he got to his deviant state, Dahmer eventually regretted his path. As his imprisonment approached, he said, "I should have never left God." Whatever he meant by that, Dahmer realized that abandoning God left his inner forces to spin out of control.

UNDER CHRIST'S CONTROL

In contrast, consider the life of Jim Elliot. He left college not with dreams of fame and fortune, but with a passion to take Christ to the headhunting Auca tribe in the Amazon jungles of Ecuador. His was a holy passion, a passion to bring redemption to this tribal people. Instead, he and four other committed, valiant young men became their victims in 1956.

Surprisingly, through the death of these five missionaries, the Aucas eventually laid down their weapons. Many of them, including the leader of the brutal attack, became Christians. Elliot had earlier revealed his inner priorities when he said, "He is no fool who gives what he cannot keep to gain what he cannot lose." Jim Elliot had discovered the real source of significance, which enabled him to direct the energies of pleasure, pride, and passion into significant, positive channels.

For many of us, careers that sustain home and family are a main focus of significance and a source of stability, security, and identity. We find value by having a place and being productive. We are affirmed for work well done and belong to a significant whole. When we are introduced the topic soon turns to, "What do you do?" We answer usually in the "doctor, lawyer, Indian chief, butcher, baker, candlestick maker" mode. To lose or fail at a career, to have to answer, "I'm out of work," is a major blow to our ego, that cocoon of significance where our inner forces reside.

After my friend Bob lost his job, I tried to be sensitive by reminding him, "Someday you'll look back and know that God had a plan and purpose in this."

His reply surprised me. "Joe, I don't see it that way. These have been the best months of my life. I've come to know Christ personally and intimately, and that gain has been worth everything to me."

For Bob, significance no longer came from a stellar career, but through a relationship with the living God. This source of significance provided him with something deeper, more stable, and more rewarding than a golden chain clamped to an executive desk.

Each of the people I've mentioned have in common their humanness. Like the rest of us they needed significance, and the inner mix of energies known as pleasure, pride, and passion drove each of them. What is not the same, however, is how they organized and managed these inner drives. Some, such as Bob, Jim Elliot, and my two minister friends, managed them well and found great gain. Others, such as Richard and Jeffrey Dahmer, trying on their own to find significance, lost it, often paying the price of personal despair and social disgrace.

OUTSIDE THE GARDEN

The contrast between gain and loss is depicted in a tense and violent moment early in the history of mankind. Two brothers, sons of Adam and Eve, chose different paths to significance. Abel lived in obedience to God. He had obviously found his significance in his relationship to God. His brother Cain lived for himself and sought to establish his own significance, yet he wanted God to endorse his self-styled worship. When God had rejected his way of life and affirmed Abel's, Cain refused to repent and instead murdered Abel, the symbol of the righteous management of life.

Cain's pleasure, pride, and passion performed in concert to obliterate this living reminder of Abel's affirmation and his rejection and loss of significance before God (Genesis 4:1–8). The outcome of Cain's action, however, was not relief but lasting regret. His life was characterized by fear and despair that hounded him for the rest of his days. Cain became the father of all those who reject the source of true significance and proudly seek to establish their own by violence in word or deed, elevating themselves at someone else's expense.

Interestingly, the parents of these two brothers set the stage for this fatal encounter by themselves falling to those three inner energies. Satan succeeded in his efforts to seduce Adam and Eve by appealing to the inner forces of pleasure, pride, and passion. His offer of the fruit of the tree of knowledge activated all three inner drives. In chapter 4 we will discuss in detail their fall and the subsequent decline of the human race, all caused by the lure of wanting personal significance.

Clearly, the actions that bubble to the surface of our lives are not lucky or unlucky expressions of a moment's chance. They are the result of dynamics that move beneath the surface, at the core of our being where systems of thought, values, dreams, and ideals are formed into actions by the surging power centers of significance: pleasure, pride, and passion. What happens in this dark yet dynamic core will determine our choices and their consequences—and ultimately, our significance—or lack thereof.

WILD STALLIONS

These three subsurface forces are like wild stallions. When harnessed, they lead to great good and significance. Unharnessed and left to run wild, however, they do major damage and leave us at best empty and at worst wasted and in despair.

Our pride, passion, and pleasure instincts move within us at a constant, untiring pace. A clear understanding of these energies is a prelude to channeling them in positive directions—directions that lead to significance rather than sorrow and loss.

PASSION

Our *passions* represent far more than our desire for sex. They include other significant desires that drive and shape us, God-given energies designed to keep us from failing our destiny. There are no truly passionless persons. True, some of us have been thwarted by disappointment and have turned stoic and cold toward life. Some of us seem rather passionless, having adopted passivity as a way of life. Yet, although some passions may be suppressed, all of us have a group of innate passions which are given to men and women alike, though sometimes in different quantity, scale, and intensity.

Passion is crucial to life. Our passions are rooted in how we are made, and, in God's divine assignment, they are designed to benefit God and society, as well as ourselves. In themselves, passions are both good and necessary.

God has placed in us at least three basic passions that provide the energy we need to be productive persons. Each of them plays a vital role in our drive for significance. One is our *passion to procreate*. In the beginning, God told Adam and Eve, "Be fruitful and increase in number; fill the earth" (Genesis 1:28a). Fewer inner energies receive more attention in our society than our sexuality. It sells products, underlies plots for soap operas, and keeps Hollywood script writers busy. It affects how we act toward each other and how we feel about ourselves. Our sexuality provides life's highest moment—the production of life itself—and is the cause of society's deepest degradations.

God also assigned us the *passion to rule* over His creation: to control, organize, and lead our environment for good. This ruling passion brings our instincts for power and authority front and center. God's assignment to Adam and Eve regarding His creation was, "Subdue it. Rule over the fish of the sea and the birds of the air and over every living creature that moves on the ground" (v. 28b).

God went on to give the first couple food for their sustenance. "I give you every seed-bearing plant on the face of the whole earth, and every tree that has fruit with seed in it. They will be yours for food" (v. 29). Each of us has a fundamental *passion for provision,* a passion that gives us the energy to gather our provision, gain satisfaction from productive work, and enjoy the fruit of our labor.

The passion for provision is one of the joys of life. I have often thought how dreadful it would be if food was unappealing to the eye and horribly distasteful. But God has made the fulfillment of our longing for food an enjoyable experience. We need food to live, and the pleasurable sights and smells associated with food as well as our hunger longing contribute to our passion to provide. If we didn't have this passion to provide, there would be no motivation to eat, and the human race would soon be annihilated.

Although the Scriptures do not specifically say that God gave us passions to energize us for these assignments, it would be strange to assume that He created us to carry out these tasks without creating the intrinsic energy and motivation to get the work done. The presence of these passions certainly are affirmed by experience.

Are there any of us who have not felt the passions of procreation, ruling, or provision? It's the rush of that first kiss which did so many funny things inside, that thought of "Who does he think he is?" when someone outpositions us, or even the passion to sneak in that extra late night snack, as innocent or fattening as it may be.

Sam Keen, in his best-selling book *Fire in the Belly,* refers to such fundamental passions when he notes that most cultures ask their men to establish mastery in the arenas of women, war, and work. He goes on to say that this is a "near universal creed linking manhood with the socially necessary activities of protecting, providing, and procreating."[1] Although Keen was writing specifically about men, such tasks were assigned equally to Adam and Eve according to Genesis 1, though the intensity and application of these passions differ between the sexes.

These primary passions lead a host of sub-passions that together energize us. Our instinct for ruling, for instance, gives rise to passions for power, position, conquest, and control. It prompts the warrior instinct and drives the subtleties of politics. It's why husbands and wives seek to rule, why parents rule their kids, why older kids are prone to boss younger, and why younger kids rule the family pet!

Meanwhile, the passion for procreation gives rise to such activities as wooing and seduction which, combined with the ruling passion, provide tremendous sexual energy that can either elevate or degrade us.

Our ruling and procreative passions create the instinct to protect. Thus, men have defended their mothers and sisters, and mothers have gathered their young into their skirts. Meanwhile, our providing instinct makes us willing to take a risk as we forage deeper into the forest to find game and, even in the face of danger, sense the excitement and thrill of the kill. That instinct drives entrepeneurs, stockbrokers, and businesspeople in the marketplace.

It means everything to be able to provide for those we love. One of our greatest senses of failure, whether man or woman, occurs when we are unable to provide. Provision gives rise to our instincts to collect and accumulate. It's the storage syndrome, the squirreling of our resources. As a child growing up in a pastor's family, I remember that we often received boxes of candy for Christmas from parishioners and friends. In our old cellar was a storage room where we kept jam and canned goods. My mother would gather all the boxes and cart them off to the cellar to keep them, as she said, "intact" for future use. It was that provision passion expressing itself in collecting. The things we accumulate are trophies of our ability to provide.

Unfortunately, our good desire to provide often expresses itself in ways that God never intended. We often work to provide an abundance of unnecessary treasures and trinkets that lead our hearts away from the Giver of it all.

As I noted, our passions are intended by God for our good and the good of others. Tragically, we often use them to advance and promote ourselves. Instead of becoming a significant contributor to my home, community, and God's glory, I become a reckless consumer of both people and things, often causing irreparable damage.

The reason is my misfocused passions. Our passions were never intended to focus on ourselves—our own pride and pleasure. They were designed to give us the energy to contribute to God's glory. Yet, deep within our soul these passions, left to themselves, run wild like untamed stallions, trampling whatever is in their path.

PRIDE

Our second inner force is pride, which drives us to establish, protect, enhance, and maintain our sense of worth. It serves to guard and promote our significance at all cost. Pride causes us to never say we're sorry, to take the credit, to belittle others, and to compete with the significance of others. It makes us seek higher and better places, establish social credentials, and claim our rights and privileges even to the detriment of those around us. Pride seeks to keep us on top and leads us on relentless searches for even higher platforms to display our significance.

If left to itself, pride will dominate every thought, every situation, every relationship, and every conversation. Clearly, it is a major detriment to an intimate and growing relationship with God. In fact, we learn from Proverbs 6:16–17 that pride is first on the list of seven things that are "detestable" to God. Anything that creates such hostility in the heart of God is serious stuff. Peter confirmed God's hostility to the proud: He "opposes the proud" (1 Peter 5:5).

Pride stimulates us to elevate ourselves above God and declare ourselves as the god of our lives. "I'll call the shots and determine my own destiny," is the motto of the proud.

Pride was one of the signature attitudes of the former heavyweight boxing champion, Muhammad Ali. His athletic success took Ali to such heights that he was once called the most recognizable athlete in the world. He proudly proclaimed, "I am the greatest," and then set out to prove it. But today, Ali is a middle-aged Parkinson's disease victim, an overweight ex-fighter whose hands shake and whose flying feet now shuffle along painfully. The most telling thing to me, however, is Ali's appraisal of his scintillating career: "I had the world," he declared recently, "and it wasn't nothin'."

We are not saying, "Kill pride." Instead we must manage this God-given energy. When our egos are directed by God's Spirit for good, we will be enthusiastic, even insistent, about God's glory. (See chapter 10 for a full discussion of "Pride Revised.")

To be properly managed, pride must hear the counsel of the psalmist, who declared, "Know that the Lord is God. It is he who has made us and not we ourselves; we are his people, and the sheep of his pasture" (Psalm 100:3). We must keep in mind the sobering warning that pride precedes a fall (Proverbs 16:18).

PLEASURE

While *pride* seeks to establish, protect, and maintain our significance, and *passion* gives us the energy for actions that promote our significance, *pleasure* is the reward that comes when we have attained the significance that our pride and passions produce. Pride and passions maneuver us toward the goal of pleasure. It's the ultimate reward.

Pleasure is so fundamental a force that the Declaration of Independence calls "the pursuit of happiness" an "inalienable" right. And as we saw in chapter 1, the Westminster Shorter Catechism recognizes that "man's chief end is to glorify God and *enjoy Him* forever" (emphasis mine). Obviously, God gave us the capacity for pleasure.

Feeling pleasure is a God-intended phenomenon. However, it can quickly move out of control. Sometimes we want pleasure more than we want God (see 2 Timothy 3:4). When He wisely calls us to sacrifice and suffer if necessary for Him, the pleasure instinct makes such devotion difficult. When our joy should be in bringing pleasure to Christ, pride and passion often turn the pleasure instinct inward so we embrace or pursue anything that offers *us* joy.

In my early days as a pastor I would begin one of my messages to teenagers by asking, "If you could choose only one of these for the rest of your life, which would it be: popularity, wealth, beauty, success, or happiness?" Without fail, these young people would overwhelmingly choose happiness. Try it on your friends. Pleasure is a powerful stallion.

It's tragic that so many pleasure palaces are in reality empty and boring once they've been experienced. Whether the pleasure is sex, money, power, position, recognition, or a host of other rewards, there is an inherent longing for more, for new thrills. For something out there not yet experienced.

The power of the pleasure search compels us in much of what we are and do.

THREE PISTONS IN AN ENGINE

The three hot forces of pleasure, pride, and passion fire in sequence like pistons in an engine, providing much of the momentum and movement in our lives. However, any misfire causes damage. These forces are a volatile mix when not under God's control.

Cain's self-motivated system of pride refused to accept humbly God's offer of worth. Cain sought to protect his false sense of significance by the passion-driven killing of Abel; he sought to elevate his own sense of significance by eliminating the one who symbolized true significance. He thought that with Abel gone, he'd finally know the pleasure of significance. But Cain's tragic mismanagement of his inner forces led to a life of insecurity, a sense of fear and despair, and a loss of significance.

Pleasure, pride, and passion focus on ourselves and our need to feel significant. Sometimes it is our passion instinct that rises, with an opportunity for pleasure kicking in and pride affirming the action. Sometimes pride leads the way, sometimes pleasure. But apart from God, they are all dedicated servants of self, and as such can never fully satisfy. As Oswald Chambers observed, "There is only one Being Who can satisfy the last aching abyss of the human heart, and that is the Lord Jesus Christ."[3]

> *Our passions, pride, and desire for pleasure are powerful motivators, bubbling to the surface in our attitudes and actions. Like the search for significance, these forces are God-given and good in themselves. But unless they are submitted to God's control, they will flow into destructive channels that not only rob us of their God-intended enjoyment, but cause us to damage ourselves and others. Just as there is no significance outside of Christ, there is no true fulfillment of these inner drives apart from Him.*

CHAPTER THREE

DOWN IN MY HEART

What people do is only the outward result of how they manage the forces that flow deep within them. This is why Jesus had so much to say about the heart, and why He was so unsparing in dealing with people who put up a good outward show of righteousness while their hearts were corrupt. If we are going to be authentic Christians, we have to see the absolute necessity of aligning our inner drives with God's purposes.

As a young man, Joseph Stalin entered a seminary in his native Georgia to study for the Russian Orthodox priesthood. But while in school he became enamored of revolutionary ideas and was constantly punished for reading forbidden books. He was finally expelled from the seminary in 1899, and left to follow the ideals of Marx and Lenin.

Rising to supreme power, Stalin led Russia through its bloodiest years of terror. The Soviet dictator murdered thousands of his countrymen—those who opposed him, those he suspected of opposing him, and even those who helped him to power. He did it all to secure the place of communism and guarantee his absolute authority. After Stalin's death, his daughter revealed that on his deathbed, he rose with his last breath to shake his fist at God.[1]

Something at the unseen center of Joseph Stalin's life seethed with anger toward God. These forces burned through to the surface, producing a dictatorship that was responsible for unparalleled human suffering and misery. The searing magma that erupted from Stalin's heart also brought about one of history's most brutal persecutions of the church. Only recently has Stalin's dream failed fully, with the collapse of communism and the breakup of the Soviet Union.

Most of us wonder how a Joseph Stalin is produced. We don't have all the answers to that question, but we know that our inner systems rarely change quickly. The incredible hardening of Joseph Stalin's heart was probably gradual, shaped by many influences. Today, those influences haven't changed much. Seductive appeals from our world all dig deep into us, mingling with the driving forces that reside just below the surface. What happens in the hidden world within us determines the actions that are plain for all to see.

THE AUTHENTIC YOU

What made Joseph Stalin so angry at God? Though we cannot say for sure, we do know one thing. Like every person, his need for significance and his pleasure, pride, and passion instincts resided in the inner core of his existence, a place the Bible calls the *heart*. The frightening reality is that the same energies that drove Stalin drive us.

The heart is the place where you dream, deliberate, decide, plot, and plan. It is the *authentic you*. The heart is what we are, stripped of the masks we wear to conform, please others, and act decently.

Unfortunately, most of us work on external conformity while we struggle with the internal energies that are programmed to move us away from God-honoring behavior. The apostle Paul demonstrated an unusually good grasp of what it means to struggle with the energies of the heart:

> I do not understand what I do. For what I want to do I do not do, but what I hate I do. And if I do what I do not want to do, I agree that the law is good. As it is, it is no longer I myself who do it, but it is sin living in me. I know that nothing good lives in me, that is, in my sinful nature. For I have the desire to do what is good, but I cannot carry it out. For what I do is not the good I want to do; no, the evil I do not want to do—this I keep on doing. Now if I do what I do not want to do, it is no longer I who do it, but it is sin living in

me that does it. So I find this law at work: When I want to do good, evil is right there with me. (Romans 7:15–21)

No wonder Paul longed for the time when this inner struggle would be no more:

> I consider that our present sufferings are not worth comparing with the glory that will be revealed in us. The creation waits in eager expectation for the sons of God to be revealed. For the creation was subjected to frustration, not by its own choice, but by the will of the one who subjected it, in hope that the creation itself will be liberated from its bondage to decay and brought into the glorious freedom of the children of God. We know that the whole creation has been groaning as in the pains of childbirth right up to the present time. Not only so, but we ourselves, who have the firstfruits of the Spirit, groan inwardly as we wait eagerly for our adoption as sons, the redemption of our bodies. (Romans 8:18–23)

This does not mean that we yield to the unbridled dictates of our hearts as we wait for a future redemptive restructuring. Our redemption from sin has an impact *now* in reversing the flow of our inner energies. In fact, the primary work of redemption is to take us who are hopelessly and helplessly separated from God—dead to Him— and *reunite* us to Him. This restores our potential to live from the inside out because we have a new heart. It enables us to know the joy of God's pleasure and avoid the empty shame that characterized us before our redemption. Paul described the old condition of our heart, and the wonder of a reunited heart, when he wrote:

> As for you, you were dead in your transgressions and sins, in which you used to live when you followed the ways of this world and of the ruler of the kingdom of the air, the spirit who is now at work in those who are disobedient. All of us also lived among them at one time, gratifying the cravings of our sinful nature and following its desires and thoughts. Like the rest, we were by nature objects of wrath. But because of his great love for us, God, who is rich in mercy, made us alive with Christ even when we were dead in transgressions—it is by grace you have been saved. And God raised us up with Christ and seated us with him in the heavenly realms in Christ Jesus, in order that in the coming ages he might show the incomparable riches of his grace, expressed in his kindness to us in

Christ Jesus. For it is by grace you have been saved, through faith—and this not from yourselves, it is the gift of God—not by works, so that no one can boast. For we are God's workmanship, created in Christ Jesus to do good works, which God prepared in advance for us to do. (Ephesians 2:1–10)

THE POWER OF CHRIST WITHIN

The life of good works, which is part of living out our redemption, required a transition from "gratifying the cravings of our sinful nature" to becoming a new creation. For "if anyone is in Christ, he is a new creation; the old has gone, the new has come!" (2 Corinthians 5:17). We live out this newness in the reality that, "I have been crucified with Christ and I no longer live, but Christ lives in me. The life I live in the body, I live by faith in the Son of God, who loved me and gave himself for me" (Galatians 2:20).

When our hearts are restructured by redemption, the old system of management dies. In its place, the heart cultivates a new pattern that puts Christ at the center of our being. He secures our sense of significance and changes the flow of our pleasure, pride, and passion, turning it toward His glory and gain.

This reality—Christ's power living freely within us—marks the difference between my former parishioner Richard, who left his wife, and my minister friends who remain faithful despite compelling opportunities to compromise their love for God and their wives. It is what separates a Jeffrey Dahmer from a Jim Elliot. Remember, both were men of passion—one letting his passions run roughshod, the other managing them for God's honor.

The capacity to make this change in our hearts begins with our redemptive *reunion* with our Creator, the only significant and completely supreme Person in the universe. This results in a redemptive *restructuring* that God wants to do in our hearts, which leads then to the redemptive *responses* that glorify God, advance His kingdom, and guarantee us a measure of genuine stability and satisfaction. They also free us from the empty regrets and loss of our pre-redemptive way of life. To know the pleasure of this way of life requires more than our reunion with God in salvation. Unfortunately, many of us attempt to go immediately from reunion to redemptive responses without undergoing the restructuring of our hearts. It's no wonder we struggle and stumble so frequently.

Before we deal with the redemptive *reunion-restructure-response* sequence of authentic significance, it's important to understand what the human heart is like in its pre-redeemed state and why.

A HYPOCRITE'S HEART

The Pharisees of Jesus' day had mastered the act of external religion, while ignoring the fact that their hearts were far from pleasing to God. Since the heart is where God meets us and resides, nothing could have been more revolting to Christ.

This is why Christ spent much of His time exposing, sometimes with scathing words, the duplicity of these men's lives. He called their rigorous religious discipline a self-serving, public display of false piety, motivated by pride. He also decried their showy prayers (Luke 18:11), their religious works performed to be seen by men, their flashy giving, and their recitation of prayers for personal praise (Matthew 6:1–5). Christ knew that their righteousness was merely a platform for their pride, pursued so passionately that they added increasingly minute laws to appear all the more righteous (which, of course, brought them great pleasure).

The Pharisees' system fed their sense of significance, but it also rendered them liable to the label *hypocrite*. Jesus exposed their hypocrisy by describing them as "whitewashed tombs" (Matthew 23:27). This was a blow to their self-gained significance, since in the Levitical code death and anything associated with it were sources of defilement. Since spiritual purity required avoiding these kinds of defilement, Christ was saying that at the very core of their being, the Pharisees were defiled.

We often think of hypocrites as those who say they believe one thing and do another. However, Scripture most often sees them as people who perform external religious acts (supposed redemptive responses) with no change (restructuring) of their hearts. Hypocrites exercise their *religion* to advance their personal significance. A Pharisee pursued perfection for the pleasure of moving up one more notch on the religious ladder.

THE PRIORITY OF THE HEART

Given the prevalent Pharisaical viewpoint, Christ spoke often about the priority of making the heart the focus of our concern. That's because our spiritual condition is measured first and foremost by our heart, not our habits. With the Pharisees listening closely, He told a crowd one day:

> "Listen to me, everyone, and understand this. Nothing outside a man can make him 'unclean' by going into him. Rather, it is what comes out of a man that makes him 'unclean.'" After he had left the crowd and entered the house, his disciples asked him about this parable. "Are you so dull?" he asked. "Don't you see that nothing that enters a man from the outside can make him 'unclean'? For it doesn't go into his heart but into his stomach, and then out of his body." (In saying this, Jesus declared all foods "clean.") He went on: "What comes out of a man is what makes him 'unclean.' For from within, out of men's hearts, come evil thoughts, sexual immorality, theft, murder, adultery, greed, malice, deceit, lewdness, envy, slander, arrogance and folly. All these evils come from inside and make a man 'unclean.'" (Mark 7:14–23)

James reiterated this truth when he reminded us that:

> When tempted, no one should say, "God is tempting me." For God cannot be tempted by evil, nor does he tempt anyone; but each one is tempted when, by his own evil desire, he is dragged away and enticed. Then, after desire has conceived, it gives birth to sin; and sin, when it is full-grown, gives birth to death. (James 1:13–15)

SPOILED BY SIN

How did our hearts become such a toxic waste dump of personal and relational corruption? We know that we were created for a significance that finds its source in God. We also were given the intrinsic energies of pleasure, pride, and passion so that those compelling forces might drive us toward full satisfaction in an unhindered relationship with God, in whose image we were made. Originally, our significance was found in a relationship with Him, our pleasure was in and from Him, our pride was focused on Him, and our passions longed for Him. This stimulated our lips to praise and our hearts to humility. From such a platform we could spontaneously declare God's glory.

Then sin entered and ravaged the scene, leaving mankind dead to God. Sin separated us totally from the source of significance, and we were left to find it apart from God. In Scripture, this fallen state of our hearts is called the "flesh," and our misguided search for pleasure, pride, and passion is often described as our "lusts." Inevitably they lead us to sorrow and loss.

Our regret and loss occur because the mad search for significance can be satisfied only in the One who created us and offers us true satisfaction. Augustine describes the sin of seeking fulfillment apart from God as a "perverse distortion." In his *The Confession of Saint Augustine*, he writes:

> Sin comes when we take a perfectly natural desire or longing or ambition and try desperately to fulfill it without God. Not only is it sin, it is a perverse distortion of the image of the Creator in us. All these good things, and all our security are rightly found only and completely in Him.[2]

Redemption through Christ *alone* reunites us with God and restores our capacity to turn from destructive and deadly pursuits to those that produce His glory and gain in our lives. But unless this process of restructuring is applied to all that we do, it will be sabotaged below the surface by the old patterns of pleasure, pride, and passion.

THE FORCES WITHIN

Understanding our struggle within requires more than knowing how our hearts got where they are. We must also understand the meaning and movements of these surgings in our soul. In chapter 2 we considered them in the setting of the Genesis creation narrative. But they are so fundamental that I want to look at them briefly again from another biblical viewpoint, that of the apostle John in 1 John 2:16.

When John wanted to describe those forces within us that are contrary to God and that drive the world around us, he isolated the three energies of our souls: passion ("the lust of the flesh"), the longing for pleasure ("the lust of the eyes"), and pride ("the boastful pride of life," NASB).

Note how the apostle qualified the use of these three energies. He warned against the lust of the flesh and the eyes and boastful pride. The problem is not with passion itself, but with passion that is misappropriated and misapplied: that is, a lust. Similarly, pride goes awry when it is focused on our own lives instead of on the God who transcends life.

Note also that although these things are "in the world," it's not the world that works against us. Rather, working against us are these energies that reside in us. What is "the world," anyway? In a sense, the world is us. The world is what it is because we are the way we are; because people are the way they are. As the cartoon character Pogo said, "We have seen the enemy, and it is us."

As noted in chapter 2, these forces help to write the stories of our lives. They are why Richard left his family; but they also help to explain a Jim Elliot, who like other men was driven by a need for significance and longings for pleasure, pride, and passion. All three longings were there, but Elliot managed them in a healthy, wholesome orientation.

You and I face the same choices as these men. We can harness these incredibly powerful forces for God's glory and our good. Or we can unharness them and let them run like those wild stallions, leaving destruction, emptiness, and despair in their path.

My *passions,* disconnected from God, long for any object or person that promises to satisfy my need for significance: a car, a companion, a title, a trip, drugs, sex, power, or position. It's different from person to person.

Pride, when not focused on God, also serves to protect, maintain, and enhance me and my significance. It promotes anything that helps the cause, from religion (the Pharisees) to lying, cheating, deceit, immorality, and lack of integrity.

Like its two companions, my *pleasure* instinct gravitates to all that makes me happy and therefore significant. One constant message from our culture is that significant people are happy, making happiness a source of significance. This gives me permission to "do it" if it makes me happy. The avoidance of sacrifice and suffering and my innate aversion to pain and problems are all part of this pleasure search. But this creates conflict within when God calls for sacrifice and suffering, or when I need to work through pain and problems to accomplish His glory.

For my friend Richard, avoiding suffering was not the issue. The lure of his affair may have been the boost to his pride as a younger woman showed interest in him. This led his passions to pour themselves into a relationship that would destroy his family and diminish his sense of worth when he faced what he had done.

It is easy for us to try and deal with these forces by despising and even denying them. But we really wouldn't want a life without any significance, pleasure, pride, or passion. Their management, not their existence, is the issue.

A POTENTIAL ERUPTION

In the field of plate tectonics, geologists study the movement of the giant rock plates that lie just beneath the earth's surface. As underground pressures build, even the slightest shifts in these massive plates can cause dramatic eruptions and movements on the surface. The more geologists study the movements of these plates, the better they understand why and how things happen above the ground. Unfortunately, scientists are unable to control the shifting plates of the earth's crust. They can only predict problems and try to prepare for the expected damage. But when the earthquake or volcanic explosion comes, the damage will still occur.

If we had no control over the forces below the crust of our lives, then we might have some excuse for our wrong actions, which may erupt at any time on the surface of our existence. But as Christians, we do have control. Paul said that sin was no longer to have mastery over us (Romans 6:14). Yet how many times have we said to ourselves and others, "That's just the way I am. I've always been this way and always will be. You'll just have to accept me like this." Then after the tremors of our behavior have shattered our world, we try to mend the cracks with all kinds of good intentions—only to have the volcano of our lives erupt again.

Thankfully, unlike the geologists who cannot change the dynamic, shifting patterns beneath the earth's surface, we can have productive and satisfying lives by setting up a biblical management of the four power brokers in our hearts. These power brokers now focus toward God's glory and gain, and not our own. In this mode of life, *the redemptive mode*, our inner energies are restored to their intended purpose, and we can know the satisfaction of living *the way we were created to live.*

But there's another mode of inner management, and it's far more prevalent. It's *the random mode*, in which our inner forces operate at will, with little rhyme or reason outside of the basic impulse *to satisfy me* and my sense of significance.

Before we can understand the strength and satisfaction of the *redemptive mode of life,* we need to look at life in the random mode and see what an empty and scattered life it really is.

> *We are all fundamentally the same. It's the outcomes of our lives that mark such dramatic differences between us. These outcomes are directly related to the way we satisfy our need for significance and manage the inner forces of passion, pride, and pleasure.*

CHAPTER FOUR

RANDOM LIVING

> *My CD player has a feature called* random. *After loading the compact discs into the player and pressing the* random *button, musical numbers are played from any track on any disc in no particular order, with no thoughtful progression or consistency. Often quiet, meditative songs are followed by fast, loud, and intense pieces. This produces an effect that can be jarring and contradictory to my sense of order and reliability.*
>
> *Unfortunately, many of us experience random living. At one moment our actions are solemn, constructive, and good; the next they're contradictory, careless, and totally inconsistent. Clearly randomness in life spells trouble.*

As a parent of three children, I have heard some interesting comments. In an attempt to describe a friend who was inconsistent and unpredictable, my son Matt once said, "Dad, the guy is really random." I thought Matt's description was colorful, and I found myself thinking about how random most of us are. A random life lacks order, consistency, and predictability. And while Matt's friend was random in nonconsequential ways, our randomness can often have serious consequences.

The inconsistency of a random life may reflect great good and great failure in the same person. Randomness is why respectable businessmen embezzle. Why otherwise revered men abuse their wives and daughters. It's why wives abandon husbands and children for other men or even other women.

Randomness is why we lose our cool on the highway or in rush-hour traffic. Why we embarrass ourselves at basketball games when our kid gets benched or unjustly whistled by the referee. Why we do things in private that contradict what we claim to be in public. It's why otherwise scrupulous people cheat on their income taxes.

At some point most of us fall into random living, even pastors and church leaders. Early in my pastoral experience, my Sunday school superintendent reminded me to order the Sunday school materials for the next quarter. "They need to be here in time for the teachers to prepare their new material." I assured him I would be delighted to do it, and immediately I forgot. I didn't procrastinate; I didn't depriori-tize it in my mind; I simply straight-out forgot. It never crossed my mind again.

The following Sunday morning I walked through the foyer with briefcase in hand containing my prepared message for the day. As I walked by the Sunday school superintendent, he asked, "Pastor, did you order the material?"

I am embarrassed to tell you—in fact I trust you won't lose all con-fidence in the future of the Moody Bible Institute—but without pre-meditation I blurted out "yes."

And as soon as that word came out of my mouth, my heart was struck with shame and guilt. Still wanting to protect my sense of sig-nificance, I walked resolutely to my office, shut my door, and opened my briefcase to review my sermon. It was randomness in its rawest form. There I was preparing to communicate the Scriptures from a God who can be nothing but truth. This morning I would stand on His behalf and be a truth-teller to the congregation. Yet I had lied to pro-tect my own significance.

The randomness did not stop there. Though the Spirit was urging me to go speak to the superintendent and his wife, who was standing next to him, and confess my fault and ask them to forgive me, my fallenness looked for a way out. *Maybe I can order it tomorrow and have it sent to the church by overnight mail.* But the nagging prompt-ing of the Holy Spirit urged me out the office door to seek to repair the damage caused by my random behavior. I asked myself, *How can I be a truth-teller when my life outside the pulpit is so different? How can I teach the sacred text and ignore its word to me?*

I began to turn the door to my office to go find this couple, and every internal energy—my pleasure, pride, and passion—tried to stay my hand. What I had defended so recklessly earlier—my significance—would now be left open and vulnerable to their perception of me as their pastor. But I had just lied to them; I had to meet with them.

At my invitation, they walked with me back into my office. I said to them, "I am committed to being the right kind of pastor to you, and you need to know that I just failed you. I not only have not ordered the material, but even worse, I have not told you the truth about it. I have wronged you and I want you to forgive me."

Thankfully, the superintendent reached out his hand and said, "Pastor, we all make mistakes. Of course I forgive you." His wife with tears puddling in her eyes assured me that she forgave me as well. It was a random moment in my life that I will never forget. The amazing quickness with which it happened and the heavy weight of regret it placed upon my soul taught me a good lesson about how important it is to reject the randomness that is driven by this obsession with our own significance.

When we engage in random living, we have allowed inner and external seductions to overturn well-managed, consistent lives. As we attempt to do whatever makes us feel significant, whether good or bad, we display major inconsistencies in our lives; thus I spoke untruth to my Sunday school superintendent the same day I prepared to declare God's truth to a church filled with truth seekers.

The person caught in randomness lacks or ignores principles that make him or her consistent and predictable. The result is a life whiplashed by a few fundamental and powerful forces that, by ourselves, we cannot control. It is the result of a life mismanaged at the core.

My wife, Martie, and I were listening to a tape by a pastor friend of ours who, with a broken spirit, was telling his congregation about the process of church discipline. He was dealing with the shocking reality of an older Christian leader who, for forty years, had been regularly sexually abusing children.

How could this be, Martie and I wondered as the recording ended. We spent a long time talking, wondering how this leader could be living a double life. We finally concluded the cause was random living —life without the principles to guide him in a consistent way.

When I was a young pastor, I watched with admiration an older pastor friend. Bob was a model of what you would want to see happen in your career track. An effective communicator of truth and zealous for the lost, he built a large congregation. His success made his name a household word in our denomination. He served on organizational boards and collected prestigious speaking engagements. He seemed confident and exuded an air of significance. What else could a person want?

He wanted the woman with whom he was counseling. He left everything for her, moving away from family and church to a no-name start in a different state.

Quite frankly, this kind of stuff makes little sense unless you understand the overwhelming power of the random mode of living. Random living is random because it is managed by my significance obsession and driven by whatever promises to bring pleasure, enhance pride, and satiate passion. Whatever starts the sequence, good or bad, will lead to behavior dictated by my obsession instead of by principles of righteousness that produce consistently good, productive results.

THE CONSEQUENCES OF RANDOM LIVING

Sometimes randomness is expressed in common, careless moments that surprise and disappoint us—leaving us ashamed of ourselves at best and destructive to others at worst.

One morning as I was driving to the office, my heart was filled with a great sense of worship and gratitude to God as I sang along with the choir on my tape deck and reveled in what my Lord means to me. As I approached the Chicago skyline, a dramatic picture in itself, the sun rose behind the buildings, a blazing ball of orange casting golden shafts of light between the buildings. Now my mind filled with thoughts of how wonderful a Creator God is. *I am His child, He is my God,* I thought.

Still reveling in worship and song, I stopped at a traffic light and noticed a taxi facing me. Its left-turn signal was on and the wheels were cocked to the left as the driver inched forward.

Now my focus changed. I knew what was in his wicked heart. He wanted to beat me across the intersection. To my shame, I have to admit that without much forethought or meditation, the inner forces in the bunker of my soul so quickly rearranged my mind and heart that when the light turned green, I nailed my accelerator and flew through the intersection to guarantee that he wouldn't beat me.

But the taxi driver did the same thing. He was making a U-turn and missed me by just a few inches. We found ourselves beside each other at the next red light. I glared at him, lifting both hands in the air with a look on my face as though to say, "What are you doing?"

But as the light turned green and I drove off, I felt shamed and disappointed that in a moment of such closeness to the Lord, I could have changed my attitude so quickly. I tried to prove my significance in that moment, but lost it to shame. I had entered the random mode; I had failed to discipline my inner life to produce what was righteous and correct when I needed it. I felt a sense of sorrow and loss.

But that wasn't all. Later, I thought of the damage my random moment could have done to the cause of Christ. I often take cabs myself. It's a necessity given the limited parking space in downtown Chicago. Quite frankly, next to our Moody Bible Institute faculty, some of the best theologians in Chicago sit behind those taxi cab wheels. The cabbie and I often end up talking about the things of the Lord.

But I knew that on this day, if that same cab driver had picked me up, I would have had no word to give him for Christ. My random behavior had victimized my witness for the Savior.

Random living, and the rubble it leaves behind, are as old as time. What a shock that Lucifer, the angel of light, the most beautiful and highly placed angel, would want to be like God, to sit on His throne. Who could have known that he would lead the most destructive rebellion in the universe?

Or who would have dreamed that Judas would sell Christ for a pocketful of change? Certainly not the other disciples, who so admired Judas that they elected him treasurer! Even after Christ handed Judas the bread, signaling that he was the betrayer, the other disciples assumed that he went out to buy supplies.

But perhaps most significant, and certainly most instructive, is the surprising and devastatingly random choice that Eve and Adam made at the front end of human history. The consequences of their sin still dictate our struggle today.

They had it all—their God and each other in a perfect, unspoiled environment. They had significance; through their relationship with God and the duties they could perform on His behalf, their lives were filled with satisfaction, meaning, productive work, and a prestigious position as governors of the entire created order. There was only one limitation, the tree of the knowledge of good and evil that stood as their opportunity to prove their love for God, who asked them not to eat of its fruit.

It's hard to believe that with all they had, Adam and Eve felt they needed more. The random moment of their sin rearranged and injured the whole Creator-created-creation experience, which will not be fully repaired until we are home in heaven.

Before we study Genesis 3 in more detail, we need to note two important facts. First and most important, God held the key players in the drama, Satan and the gardeners of Eden, fully accountable for their actions. Second, they not only suffered the consequences of their randomness, but many others had to take a hit for their choices, as well. Randomness is never victimless.

Even random behavior in private affects those who live around the edges of our lives. Private experiences with pornography alter a man's perception of the value of women. Pornography can redefine his expectations of his wife, and can become so addictive that the habit begins to dictate how the man spends his time and money.

Christ warned us that random thoughts soon show up in our words and works (Matthew 12:33–37). Words and works are never spoken or done in a vacuum. Bitterness harbored, for instance, creates all kinds of upheaval in relationships (Hebrews 12:15). Random works of hidden cheating and dishonesty erode trust and breed a spirit of deception and suspicion that will cripple us in the workplace and at home.

Unfortunately, we live in a society that denies personal responsibility for bad actions and discounts talk of consequences. We are responsible, however, and there will be consequences for living in the random mode.

THE RANDOM SEQUENCE

As Genesis 3 unfolds, Satan approaches Eve at a strategic and extremely vulnerable level: her core need for significance. He plants doubt about God's Word in her, casts a shadow over God's goodness and motives, then goes for the jugular and offers Eve more significance than she has in God. In fact, he offers a *new* significance *apart* from God. "When you eat of it your eyes will be opened and you will be like God, knowing good and evil" (v. 5).

THE SEDUCTION OF SIGNIFICANCE

We have seen how fundamental our need for significance is, and the tremendous power it has to manipulate us when we are empowered by the inner energies of passion, pride, and pleasure. What is so intriguing about Genesis 3 is that Eve was already significant as a person. She had unqualified acceptance and fellowship with God, and she enjoyed His affirmation. She and Adam were the pinnacle of His creative work. Professor and author Larry Crabb describes their situation:

> Before the Fall Adam and Eve were both significant and secure. From the moment of their creation their needs were fully met in a relationship with God unmarred by sin. Significance and security were attributes or qualities already resident within their personalities, so they never gave them a second thought. When sin ended their innocence and broke their relationship with God . . . [Adam] now was wrestling with threatened insignificance.[1]

Eve was also fulfilled in her relationship to Adam and enjoyed the sense of worth that came from completing him. Without her, it was "not good" for Adam (2:18)—the only time in the entire creation sequence that God said this. Adam and Eve enjoyed a sense of significance that has not been equaled since.

Yet with all this, Satan still was able to begin the fall of the human race by telling Eve that she *wasn't quite significant enough;* he offered her the added significance of being like God, and she accepted. Now she would have to step across the line of loyalty and obedience to God. In so doing she—and Adam—turned their backs on secured significance.

Fewer seductions are more powerful than the seduction of significance—whether we feel insignificant or have achieved great significance as Eve and Adam did.

Satan used the tree of the knowledge of good and evil as the point of appeal to Eve. It's no accident that the Scripture records the tree's eye-catching appeal for Eve. It was pleasing to the eye, but that wasn't the issue. The issue was God's command not to touch the tree. Neither Adam nor Eve had any reason to eat. They lacked nothing, yet they disobeyed. They really doubted they had enough.

Things haven't changed all that much. The world around us is still full of seductive lures to significance. These external forces beckon us to eat of their fruit and satisfy our craving for worth and value.

We've already talked about these lures, whether material things, sex, corporate power and position, or social status. As they move across the surface of our lives, the radar screen of our souls picks up the signal and alerts the control center to an opportunity for the "me" down there to pull the levers in response, to use these allurements in some scheme to satisfy our soulish longings for significance. When we do, we abandon our loyalty to God and show ourselves unsatisfied with what we have in God.

The sequence of Adam and Eve's random response illustrates the power of this kind of appeal, which sets in motion an overwhelming flow of inner forces. Without a disciplined system of management, these forces result in randomness.

As I drove to work on the morning I described earlier, the sight of that taxi with its turn signal blinking registered an alert in my soul that interrupted my glorious moment of worship. The stranger gunned his engine and my ego was engaged. Like a "code blue" alert in a hospital that overrides normal functions and focuses the energies of the hospital staff on the emergency, my inner self refocused in an amazingly quick and random response.

The "Who does he think he is?" side of my significance need alerted my pride. That fired up my passion to overcome, and my pleasure side assured me that beating that taxi through the intersection would be far more pleasing than being taken advantage of. All systems were go in my command center, telling me to pull the "foot-accelerator" lever and overcome this threat to my right-of-way—to maintain and defend my significance. All this happened as the taped choir sang praises through my car speakers. Surrounded by sounds of praise and worship of God, I looked to advance my significance.

THE APPEAL TO OUR INNER FORCES

In Eve's situation, it is important to note that the external seduction to significance—the tree—also appealed to her inner instincts of passion, pride, and pleasure.

Genesis 3:6 says Eve saw that the tree was "good for food." It appealed to her inner longing for provision. It wasn't that she needed food. But it was an external seduction linked to an internal *passion*.

She then realized that it was a *delight* to the eyes. It would be a source of *pleasure*. And she believed it would make her wise, a function of her inner force of *pride*. As these energies merged with the opportunity to advance her significance, she reached out and ate.

And Adam followed. Perhaps he believed the same lie and felt the surging energies in his soul. Or, perhaps he had come to feel that Eve was the source of his significance, given that their love and intimacy must have flourished in the unhindered environment of Eden. He may have eaten to preserve a bond with her even at the risk of breaking his bond with God.

How often we neglect or violate our commitment to Christ because our significance has found its source in something other than Him. Whether it's a friend, spouse, career, or an opportunity for increased significance, when the fruit is offered we take it. Nice girls from upstanding homes violate the moral code they know is right and break their fellowship with God to keep a dating relationship in which their partner is willing to eat the fruit. Businessmen who are leaders at church and good fathers and husbands violate principles of integrity in the marketplace where the boss and his colleagues are eating the fruit. The thought of turning down the "garden snack" and threatening their position, or possibly even their career, is overwhelming because that's where so much of their significance is experienced.

Our obsession with advancing, maintaining, defending, and promoting our significance leaves us vulnerable to the world's seductive appeal to our inner forces. When they begin to move through us, it's not surprising that we feel an overwhelming urge to answer their call. Since our choice is being manipulated by the realities of the moment, the result is erratic patterns of behavior so typical of the random mode of living.

It's not always the allure of that which is wrong that triggers a random response. For instance, early on in human history the passion for provision led our ancestors out to fish. Nothing wrong with that passion, of course; it's necessary for survival. One day, though, a fisherman pulled in the biggest fish that had ever been caught. His pride kicked in and his catch became not a meal but a trophy. The fisherman chose to forego his need for food to merely display his skills by showcasing the catch. Others then went fishing, quietly hoping that they might catch a bigger fish yet and know the pride and pleasure that would come from being the best fisherman in the village.

Similarly, for people in the marketplace it's not always the pleasure of making money to provide that stimulates the excitement. It's the thrill of the kill. This explains why books like Donald Trump's *The Art of the Deal* are national bestsellers. The thrill of getting the contract, the promotion, or the glory begins to eclipse the intended purpose of our passion to provide.

The different ways that men and women respond also tend to confuse and complicate these urges. My brother-in-law, Larry, is an avid hunter who never misses the opportunity to go into Upper Michigan with his friends when deer season opens. One winter, he bagged two large bucks with nice racks of antlers. Normally, Larry and his buddies dress out the kill before they come home and put the venison in freezer boxes.

But Larry was struck with the trophy-size of the antlers, so he decided to tie both deer on his truck and bring them home for his wife, Kelsey, to see. No doubt he expected that when he got home she would run out and fall into his arms, marveling at the way her great hunter had provided for his family's needs. After all, he would not mount their heads; he was providing food. To his amazement, when he pulled into the driveway Kelsey came out, looked at him, and said, "Larry, why did you bring these home?" Her nurturing instincts prompted deep feelings for the deer and shock at her husband's actions. What Larry thought would be heralded as significant his wife disavowed, for her inner urgings were working out a wholly different agenda.

A TEMPORARY GOOD

Sometimes, the random mode of living produces results that at first blush appear to be good. For instance, a woman may host a meeting in her home for a political candidate, helping her neighbors to learn about local issues, to ask questions, and even to find encouragement. They may even compliment her for helping them think through the issues. But she may do so because she enjoys the attention, the influence, and being in control. She loves speaking and leading, and the meetings stoke her fire for personal significance and power. Similarly, some may be drawn into something noble such as the ministry because the limelight, acclaim, and power appeal to their need for significance and their passion, pride, and pleasure. Even so, some people may be blessed and built up by his ministry.

Unfortunately, those who serve with such motives are ultimately driven to manage their lives and ministries from prideful perspectives. In church ministry, for example, this random mode is ultimately destructive as the minister serves himself rather than serving Christ and His church. The congregation and staff will soon feel manipulated, controlled, used—and in some cases, abused. One source of potential danger is counseling. If a pastor who is obsessed with his significance meets a vulnerable counselee, the pastor himself will be vulnerable to a major fall.

A fellow minister called me some time ago to ask about a large and influential church that he hoped would call him to be their pastor. I asked him why he wanted to leave his present charge and go there to serve. His response? "I hope to have a national writing, speaking, and radio ministry, and I feel that this type of church could help me launch them." Somehow I knew that here was trouble looking for a place to happen.

People may give to the church, missions, and charity because it makes them feel significant to be so "good." Many do their giving in very public ways to satisfy their pride and pleasure instincts. Christ reproved the Pharisees for giving, and praying, in public not because giving and praying are wrong, but because they did it for the wrong reasons.

Giving to God is an opportunity to advance His significance and that of His work, not our own. Our randomness will soon show if self-advancement is our motive. As soon as something else appears that promises more fulfillment than giving to God and His work, the random person will put his money on that boat, car, house, or whatever it is that feeds his significance.

This randomness is why some people pray eloquently in public and never in private. Why we say wonderful things to one another's faces and horrible things behind one another's backs. When we manage our lives through an obsession with our own significance and through inner drives that lack a consistent sense of direction, we end up in a whiplash sort of existence.

GETTING OUR SUSPENDERS CAUGHT

It reminds me of the man on a moped who pulls up at a red light next to a Porsche. The driver rolls down his window and challenges the moped rider to a drag race. The rider declines politely, but the

Porsche driver insists. He finally appeals to the moped rider's sense of significance by saying, "Look, you can tell all of your friends that you dragged a Porsche."

That did it. The man on the moped agrees, the light turns green, and they are off. The Porsche is down the road in a flash, but as the driver glances in his rearview mirror he sees the moped coming at him with increasing speed. It screams past him, getting smaller and smaller in the distance in front of him.

Then the shocked driver sees the moped coming back toward him, screaming by him in the opposite direction and getting smaller and smaller in his rearview mirror. But then the moped starts coming toward him again, and with surprising speed whips by in front of him. At the next light, the Porsche driver leans out of his window, looks the moped over, and asks incredulously, "What kind of engine have you got in that machine?"

Out of breath, with fear all over his face, the moped rider says, "Not much of one, but do you mind if I unhook my suspenders from your side mirror?"

That's pretty much what life will be like for us until we unhook our "suspenders" from our obsession with significance and the out-of-control energies in our souls. Without the redemptive mode of inner management in place, we'll be whiplashed back and forth by every seduction that pulls up next to us and rolls down its window.

Even the best actions of the random mode (for example, charity, Christian service, kind words, acts of compassion) also feed pride and fuel pleasure as we enjoy our works of the flesh and seek recognition from others. We can even feed a surge of pride by remaining anonymous in our charity and then feeling noble about it!

Ultimately, the sinful expressions of random living produce nothing that is wholly good, safe, and productive. There will always be some mixture of self-serving advantage and resultant loss. As we saw in chapter 3, the apostle James taught us that when our behavior is stimulated by self-interest, it results in sin and death (James 1:13–16).

Interestingly, for Eve and Adam the consequences were most fully felt within. They remind us that our attempts to enhance our significance actually bring shame and the loss of personal significance, dignity, and worth. Adam and Eve were now aware of and ashamed of their nakedness (Genesis 2:25; 3:7). They tried to regain what they had lost by their own efforts. Fig leaves were the first human attempt to recover "significance lost" after Adam and Eve had suffered "paradise lost."

At the very heart of it, random living is simply the effort to satisfy our hunger for a significance that has been severed from its only true source of fulfillment. Apart from God, all of our "fig leaf" attempts at life result in some measure of sorrow, loss, and regret.

It may be the result of trying to sew together the fig leaves of power, position, and prosperity. Or it may be the tragic effects of a fig-leafed life littered with broken relationships and people victimized by our search for significance. As it did with Eve and Adam, the random mode of living always backfires by reducing our sense of worth.

SYSTEMS OF OBSESSION

Interestingly, random responses can become a way of life. Think of the times when we are threatened by someone's words, which leads us to resort to louder, more threatening words in return. If we discover that this response seems to preserve our significance, feed our pride, and defend our worth, we will log this pattern in our internal command center and resort to it time and time again.

In this way random people become somewhat predictable, though not for righteousness! They build a system of response that temporarily satisfies their inner needs. Thus, they are motivated to replay this "tape" as often as possible until a habit pattern is formed.

In a cruel twist of our fallenness, these habits can become addictive, automatically triggering our response when we don't want to, don't enjoy it, and know that it's destroying us. Addictions are destructive, unreasonable urgings in our soul whose power eclipses reason and extends risk beyond the limits of safety. They may have begun rather innocently in response to our need for significance, energized by our pleasure, pride, and passion. But feeding on these instincts, a monster develops within that now handles the controls, leaving us nearly helpless in that area of our randomness.

BACK TO EGYPT

Let's return to Joseph, one of Israel's twelve sons who remains a classic example of a person who rejected life in the random mode. His way of living was entirely different, motivated by faith in a God who secured the young slave's significance.

As we recall the daily attempts by Potiphar's wife to seduce him, we need to remember that the Egyptians prided themselves in beautiful, sensual women. Joseph was in the prime of youth and far from any restraining influence. A random man would have fallen in a minute. How significant to be desired by the boss's wife, especially since Joseph was little more than a slave. What a compelling appeal to passion, pride, and pleasure. His steadfast refusal to abandon God to gain more than he was intended to have is outward evidence that he was not a slave to an inner need for significance. His refusal demonstrates that, with God's help, it is possible to manage our inner drives to withstand the alluring seductions on the outside.

Breaking the grip of random living begins by redirecting our search for significance and satisfying pleasure, pride, and passion in safe and productive ways. God offers us the ability to reprogram our lives and build patterns and habits that will bless and benefit Him, ourselves, and those around us. He desires to replace the random mode with His redemptive mode of living, which is an outgrowth of our reunion with Him and its secured significance.

Before we can take hold of God's redemptive pattern, however, we must recognize and deal with our desire to have more—more of the things on the other side of loyalty to God. As we shall see, most of us will struggle with the allure of more.

> *We've all experienced random moments—those haphazard, reckless decisions that get us into all sorts of trouble. But randomness is much more than a harmless trait of youthful days. It often becomes a predictable and destructive way of life.*
>
> *The sin that plunged our race into chaos was the result of a random choice in Paradise—a choice that appealed to their desire for more. Though Adam and Eve had more than they needed, the allure of still more proved to be their fatal flaw.*

CHAPTER FIVE

THE MADNESS OF MORE

Why are so few of us, even as Christians, genuinely content? Though Christ calls us to contentment in Him, the compulsion of more constantly threatens to pull us away from God. Many of us fall into empty searches for a significance that more cannot supply.

Liberation from this compulsion comes when we understand the source of these desires for more.

The Broadway musical that recreated the Charles Dickens classic, *Oliver Twist*, opens in an orphanage dining room with young Oliver holding his empty bowl, appealing to the stern orphanage director, "Please sir, I want some more."

The irritated director snarls, "More!" He then yells, "Catch him! Snatch him! . . . Pick him up and bounce him. Wait! Before we put the lad to task. May I be so curious as to ask his name?"

The chorus breaks out, "Oliver! Oliver! Never before has a boy wanted more. . . . He will curse the day somebody named him Oliver."[1] Everything would have been fine for Oliver Twist if he'd simply been

1. "Oliver" is from the Columbia Pictures–Romulus Film *Oliver!* Words and music by Lionel Bart. © Copyright 1960 (Renewed) Lakeview Music Co. Ltd., London, England. TRO–Hollis Music, Inc., New York, controls all publications rights for the USA and Canada. Used by permission.

content with what he had. What he wanted was more, and what he got was trouble.

Oliver is a symbol for our lives as well. Wanting more typically brings trouble, from the need to maintain more possessions to financial pressure from overused credit cards, all due to our addictive appetites to acquire.

We can't deal fully with our significance obsession until we understand how easily the madness of more seduces us. Like a mirage in the desert, our thirst for more can drive us to fantasies of significance apart from God. The obsession with more can distort every aspect of our lives, from relationships to families.

A UNIVERSAL CRAVING

None of us is free from the inner search for more. It may be the unending search for more significance, more pleasure, more satisfaction of our passions, or more platforms for our pride. This urge for more is seduced by opportunities all around us for more: more power, more possessions, more money, and more fame. Even the craving for more peace and comfort can consume us.

While these beckoning mirages of more in life's desert may not be wrong in and of themselves, denying ourselves contentment to follow their allure can lead to peril and loss.

BIG BITES

I have a friend whose hobby is sailing. He tells me that sailors suffer from a malady called "five-foot fever." Once a sailor has a boat for a while, he begins thinking, "What I really need is a boat about five feet longer." Interestingly, my friend says that "five-foot fever" afflicts those with eighty-foot yachts as badly as it does those with twelve-foot runabouts. Complicating the malady is the fact that marinas are full of bigger and better boats, giving rise to the thought, "I could be more satisfied if I had a little bigger and better boat." Unfortunately, no matter how big your boat is, the insatiable monster of more keeps troubling you for more.

We see this madness played out all the time in the lives of today's "stars." According to Timothy Morgan, rock singer Ozzy Osbourne said that as soon as he became a millionaire, he wanted to be "a double millionaire." But as Morgan observes, "Envy and avarice are self-defeating in the end."[2]

This madness helps explain why lotteries are so appealing. A recent commercial for the Illinois state lottery captured its lure. The TV commercial was almost obscene in its seductive invitation for people to risk their hard-earned income on an improbable windfall. The commercial depicted an elderly couple sitting on their front porch, obviously without much money or much to do. They begin dreaming of a cruise and of dancing under the starry sky.

The commercial spun out their dreams, then moved to an obviously poor man standing at a bus stop. He too begins to dream of a better life, with his own car and more of the things he longed for. The message, of course, was that all of this awaited anyone who would buy a lottery ticket at the nearest store. The commercial implied they could have more—much more, if they won the minimum $5 million in the state lottery.

The obscenity of that commercial is its appeal to the elderly and the poor, people who can least afford to gamble on the lottery, but who are most vulnerable to its seduction. The creators of that commercial are preying on the weakest elements of society, knowing that regardless of who we are or what our station in life, the madness within us for more is a driving force. The trouble is that even those very few who strike it rich in the lottery often find life less satisfying than when they were "normal" people, living contentedly with what they had.

SMALL BITES

Sometimes it's not big things like boats and bucks that eat at us. Sometimes the madness nibbles away at us in small bites. Advertisers are well aware that we are vulnerable to this seduction. Many products are marketed as "new" or "better," giving you the impression that what you now have is inferior.

Car makers know they can make a killing by adding a few more "bells and whistles" to a car and then selling them as options at a high profit margin. Recently I was in a car dealership asking my friend, who is a salesman there, what next year's model would be like. He said it was basically the same as the current model, but would have seat warmers, a retractable coffee cup holder built into the arm rest, and a few new colors of paint.

What I found interesting was what happened inside me as I listened to him. If it hadn't been for a dose of biblical sanity, those small changes would have been very appealing to me, given the cold winters in Chicago and my addiction to coffee. I was surprised at how alluring those little bites of "more" really were. Those "bonus features" had a way of making me feel discontented with my car. *If only it had a little more,* I heard myself saying.

It doesn't take much to upset our contentment and sidetrack us from the pursuit of character and Christlikeness to the stockpiling of that which is new, bigger, better, or more convenient.

BIG TROUBLE

Sometimes the trouble with more is measured in drastic consequences. Our lack of satisfaction with what we have can erode our commitment to the priorities that should be primary in our lives. Our culture has lured many into the marketplace not out of necessity, which sometimes is the case, but out of a craving for more. More significance. More cash. More fulfillment. Dad and Mom go their separate ways after a quick cup of coffee, stress themselves out in the corporate jungle, only to return at night tired and tense with no energy or desire to build a deep and intimate relationship.

How much better if one spouse would make the home a pleasant and safe haven, while the other spouse produced the income. The issue is complicated by a culture that depicts homemakers as dependent underachievers. And even if a couple is able to manage dual careers and build a godly relationship, what about their children? What happens when parents—who for reasons of more—drop children off at the day care center, pick them up in the evening, then try to nurture them in the few last hours of the day when everyone is tired and strained? Sadly, at the end of it all what appeared to be more ends up as less—and loss.

I'm reminded of the story of the big dog who was trotting home one day, a fine steak firmly in his jaws. Happy with his fresh find, he crossed a little foot bridge and stopped to look in the water, where he saw his reflection. He supposed the vision to be another dog with a steak in its mouth. In the distortion of the reflecting pond, the dog assumed that the other dog's steak was better than his. When he opened his mouth to grab it, his steak disappeared into the pond. Just when the dog thought he had more, he ended up with less.

Another complication to our madness for more is a unique brand of heresy that's touted every day over the religious airwaves and in massive conferences across the country. It may just be the most malicious appeal of all to a Christian's compulsion for more. It is the brazenly proclaimed teaching that says if you just have enough faith, God will give you health, wealth, and happiness. *He has to*, say the false prophets of more. He's bound by His promises to prosper you. All you have to do is claim your inheritance—after, of course, you have sent these false teachers your "seed gift" to guarantee your return from God.

This teaching is detestable because it allows us to cover our greed with a cloak of faith, giving us permission to demand from God those things that He may want to give us, but has never promised to. Ironically, the teaching often comes from those who are driven by their own madness for more. Furthermore, it distorts faith and God's work of grace in a person who has learned to be content.

A FOOLISH SEARCH

Whether we listen to the blandishments of the health and wealth preachers, the advertisers of Madison Avenue, or the personal inner seductions of our pride, pleasure, and passion, when we live to satisfy our hunger for significance apart from contentment in Christ, we demonstrate that we really believe that life is found in more, regardless of our rhetoric. Jesus has called us to be "rich to God" (Luke 12:21); but our distorted values are like those of the man who had stored wealth in his barns. In chapter 1, we looked at the wealthy man briefly; let's revisit him in Luke 12, beginning a few verses before the story of the foolish farmer.

In verse 13, a man asked Christ for a favor. As the crowd moved along, this man no doubt strained to catch Christ's attention. Finally, he found Christ's eyes fixed on his and blurted out, "Teacher, tell my brother to divide the inheritance with me."

Now that's a life out of focus. He had the undivided attention of the Son of God! He could have talked with the Savior about the profound realities of life and eternity. He could have asked Jesus to bless his frail humanity. Instead, he asked for bucks, his piece of the pie. This man is an everlasting metaphor of the obsession with consumption that is such a compelling force in all of us. Jesus' answer was brutally honest and intensely profound: "Watch out! Be on your guard against all kinds of greed; a man's life does not consist in the abundance of his possessions" (v. 15). He then went on to contrast the madness of more with the values of eternity:

And he told them this parable: "The ground of a certain rich man produced a good crop. He thought to himself, 'What shall I do? I have no place to store my crops.' "Then he said, 'This is what I'll do. I will tear down my barns and build bigger ones, and there I will store all my grain and my goods. And I'll say to myself, "You have plenty of good things laid up for many years. Take life easy; eat, drink and be merry."' But God said to him, 'You fool! This very night your life will be demanded from you. Then who will get what you have prepared for yourself?' "This is how it will be with anyone who stores up things for himself, but is not rich toward God." (vv. 16–21)

Christ said the same things this way in Mark 8:36–37: "What good is it for a man to gain the whole world, yet forfeit his soul? Or what can a man give in exchange for his soul?" There is something far more important than the more of this world: It is the more of Jesus Christ. In Him and Him alone we can be fully content.

Yet, even those of us who have trusted Christ to cancel hell and guarantee heaven for us, who have not gained the world and lost our souls, still struggle with putting the issue of more in its proper place. Isn't it interesting that Judas betrayed Christ for thirty more pieces of silver? While it is uncertain whether Judas was a genuine follower of Christ, the principle holds that even His true followers still have the capacity to betray His leadership and the principles of His Word for bigger bags of silver.

How easy it is to deny the demands of biblical stewardship because we want to spend our money on something more for us instead of something more for His kingdom. That's a betrayal of His work in us. How easy it is to betray Him in our relationships when we seek greater significance through power plays that give us more control, How ready we are to betray the work of Christ in us to find more satisfaction for our passions. Our addiction to more does more than cause us difficulty and disillusionment. It also leads us to imperil that which is most valuable and significant to us, our fellowship with Christ.

THE CURE FOR OUR MADNESS

Those who are stuck with little and have limited capacity to gain more are not immune to these temptations. Periodically, I observe that some of us who don't have much take pleasure in our lack of abundance, thinking it proves that we are obviously free from covetousness and the compulsion to consume. However, we often dislike those who have been blessed with more. We look at them with a sense of spiritual disdain and pride ourselves in being more spiritually significant than they are. Our thinking goes like this: *I have a more simple life. I can focus on the spiritual while they spend their time stockpiling goods. I'll grow with God.* Our thoughts ignore the possibililty that these followers of Christ may have been sovereignly blessed by God so that they might have much to share (1 Timothy 6:18).

Unfortunately, this attitude only reveals our covert covetousness, buried deep in our soul. The secret wish to have more may be the very impulse that drives us to dislike those who do have more. And given the chance, we'd become adequate consumers ourselves.

DRAGONSLAYER

Ancient mythology pictures manhood in the image of a knight in shining armor, with sword drawn and foot on the chest of a huge fire-breathing dragon. Indeed, one Christian martyr known as Saint George was wrapped in legend as having slain a dragon to rescue the king's daughter, Sabra. Though Saint George was an actual person living in the third century, the legends beginning centuries after his death resulted in a painting depicting his alleged heroics, as well as the recounting in the *Golden Legend.* Here is the highest accomplishment of manhood—to singlehandedly defeat a beast and rescue a fainting maiden from a dragon's grasp.

It's time for some modern, genuine feats of courage to rescue ourselves and others from the dragon called More's Peril.

The apostle Paul prescribed the deliverance from this madness in his classic instructions to Timothy. First Timothy 6 details how we fatally wound this dragonian threat. How do we cure this madness and slay the dragon? We begin by leaving the perilous pursuit of significance apart from God for pursuits far grander. We pursue three things: *contentment,* which is not found in the more of material things but in the more of Christ (vv. 6–8); *character,* which is the richness of authentic Christian living (vv. 10–11); and *contribution,* the commitment to give, not get. Let's look at each of these.

CONTENTMENT

Paul gave us the timeless ingredients for true gain when he said that "godliness with contentment is great gain" (1 Timothy 6:6). He then urged Timothy to cultivate contentment with the essentials of life (v. 8).

Authentic Christianity demands that we live in the peaceful context of contentment. We pursue contentment primarily because the madness of more is such a serious threat to an authentic and prosperous relationship with God.

Covetousness is Scripture's word for our obsessive compulsion for more. Covetousness is the adversary. How serious is it? So serious that God issued a prohibition against it in His list of Ten Rules that chart the history of righteous behavior (Exodus 20:17). Throughout Scripture, covetousness is viewed as a debilitating illness that blocks the fullness of God in our lives.

As we seek more of possessions we seek less of Him. Wanting more of things that wear out and are temporal crowds out our wanting more of Him who is ever fresh and eternal. As Christ warned, "You cannot serve God and money" (Matthew 6:24).

Striving for more is also rebuked in Christ's teaching on kingdom priorities to disciples who were worried about what they would wear and eat. In Luke 12:22–34, following the lesson of the foolish farmer, Christ reminded them—and reminds us—that God is concerned about the more in our lives and that our trust should be in Him for what we need:

> Therefore I tell you, do not worry about your life, what you will eat; or about your body, what you will wear. Life is more than food, and the body more than clothes. Consider the ravens: they do not sow or reap, they have no storeroom or barn; yet God feeds them. And how much more valuable you are than birds! Who of you by worrying can add a single hour to his life? Since you cannot do this very little thing, why do you worry about the rest? Consider how the lilies grow. They do not labor or spin. Yet I tell you, not even Solomon in all his splendor was dressed like one of these. If that is how God clothes the grass of the field, which is here today, and tomorrow is thrown into the fire, how much more will he clothe you, O you of little faith! And do not set your heart on what you will eat or drink; do not worry about it. For the pagan world runs after all such things, and your Father knows that you need them. (vv. 22–30)

Here is a clear call to realign our compulsion to consume. Jesus concluded by calling us to "Seek his kingdom, and these things will be given to you as well. Do not be afraid, little flock, for your Father has been pleased to give you the kingdom" (vv. 31–32). With a promise like that, contentment shouldn't be our problem!

But Jesus went a step further. The mark of true contentment is a *willingness* to divest ourselves of what we have when we have an opportunity to stockpile treasures in heaven: "Sell your possessions and give to the poor. Provide purses for yourselves that will not wear out, a treasure in heaven that will not be exhausted, where no thief comes near and no moth destroys. For where your treasure is, there your heart will be also" (vv. 33–34).

R. C. Sproul is right when he says, "Modern man has an aching void. The emptiness we feel cannot be relieved by one more gourmet meal or another snort of cocaine. We carry water in a sieve when we try to fill the empty space with a better job or a bigger house."[3]

Paul knew what this kind of contentment felt like. He wrote to the church at Philippi, thanking them for the money that they had sent to him, explaining that he had not longed for more, but rather:

> I rejoice greatly in the Lord that at last you have renewed your concern for me. Indeed, you have been concerned, but you had no opportunity to show it. I am not saying this because I am in need, for I have learned to be content whatever the circumstances. I know what it is to be in need, and I know what it is to have plenty. I have learned the secret of being content in any and every situation, whether well fed or hungry, whether living in plenty or in want. I can do everything through him who gives me strength. (Philippians 4:10–13)

The key that we so often miss in this passage is the apostle's concluding statement that the capacity to be content regardless of material supply is found in Christ. This may also open a window on the observation that is made in Hebrews 13:5–6:

> Keep your lives free from the love of money and be content with what you have, because God has said, "Never will I leave you; never will I forsake you." So we say with confidence, "The Lord is my helper; I will not be afraid. What can man do to me?"

The focus of our contentment needs to be our confidence that Christ is all that He says He is, that He is aware of and will supply our needs, and that if we have Him, we have enough.

In Psalm 73, the psalmist lamented how *much* the pagans around him had, compared with the scarcity of his life. His lament even brought him to a point of spiritual despair when he declared, "This is what the wicked are like—always carefree, they increase in wealth. Surely in vain have I kept my heart pure; in vain have I washed my hands in innocence" (vv. 12–13).

His spiritual disillusionment with the lessness of his life was only remedied when he "entered the sanctuary of God; then I understood their final destiny" (v. 17). He confessed that his obsession with consumption had rendered him senseless and ignorant (v. 22), and he then resolved his inner struggle by proclaiming God's sufficiency: "Yet I am always with you; you hold me by my right hand. You guide me with your counsel, and afterward you will take me into glory" (vv. 23–24).

No wonder the psalmist then exclaimed with joy, confidence, and fulfillment:

> Whom have I in heaven but you? And being with you, I desire nothing on earth. My flesh and my heart may fail, but God is the strength of my heart and my portion forever. Those who are far from you will perish; you destroy all who are unfaithful to you. But as for me, it is good to be near God. I have made the Sovereign Lord my refuge. I will tell of all your deeds. (vv. 25–28)

CHARACTER

A second clear principle from 1 Timothy 6 that liberates us from the madness of more is this: We must never compromise character in order to gain more. Paul said that some who longed for wealth had "wandered from the faith and pierced themselves with many griefs" (v. 10). But Timothy was to "flee from all this, and pursue righteousness, godliness, faith, love, endurance and gentleness" (v. 11).

Let's go back to two of our earlier "case studies" from Scripture that are highly instructive here. Lucifer was the most powerful angel in all the created host. Adam and Eve had been given the overwhelming abundance of Eden. We could assume that all three had more than enough to keep themselves content. Yet, the message of their lives is clear. When it comes to attempts to find significance and satisfaction apart from God, enough is never enough. In both cases, a longing for personal significance was fatal when sought in having more than the

Creator had provided. To find significance, they each compromised their character.

For Lucifer, it was the compelling force of pride that drove him to try and make himself like God. Isaiah recounted Lucifer's fall:

> How you have fallen from heaven, O morning star, son of the dawn! You have been cast down to the earth, you who once laid low the nations! You said in your heart, "I will ascend to heaven; I will raise my throne above the stars of God; I will sit enthroned on the mount of assembly, on the utmost heights of the sacred mountain. I will ascend above the tops of the clouds; I will make myself like the Most High." But you are brought down to the grave, to the depths of the pit. (Isaiah 14:12–15)

All of Lucifer's significance was not enough for him unless he could become as God.

We've already noted the desire of Eve and Adam for the one thing that was withheld from them. The obsession with more significance, "You will be like God" (Genesis 3:5), was a compelling seduction to Eve, channeled through the forces of more pleasure, passions fulfilled, and pride satisfied. But just when Eve thought that more would satisfy, she gained shame and loss.

Several observations are critical at this point. First, God had seen fit to give Lucifer, Adam, and Eve an abundant supply of beauty, power, and position. God met all their needs, but when Lucifer intimated that Eve should want more, her heart was distracted from fullfillment in God. The gifts did satisfy Adam and Eve's needs, though Eve began to think she should want more. That was God's sovereign design for them, as it is for many in our day. The challenge is not in how much we have, but rather in finding God sufficient in the midst of what we have.

It is also important to note that these three experienced not only shame and loss, but judgment when they crossed the line of allegiance to God to gain what they didn't have. The issue then becomes not what we have, but how we got what we have. It's called *character*.

Note too that it was not a throne or a piece of fruit that compelled them to compromise God's Lordship in their lives. Those were only physical manifestations of their inner cravings. It was their longing for significance through pleasure, pride, and passion that made the more on the other side of the line so attractive. According to Paul, those who "want to get rich" (1 Timothy 6:9) also cross the line and destroy themselves.

We cannot miss that the result of Adam and Eve's attempt at gain outside the scope of godliness brought loss not only to them, but to the whole human race. This is the madness of more, whether it is more significance at the expense of someone else's significance, more quenching of our passion to the detriment of others, more promotion of our pride to the humiliation of those around us, or more seeking for pleasure at the cost of another's pain.

Why is the lure of more so compelling? Obviously our fallen nature —our sinfulness—is a major reason. But our pursuit of more goes deeper than that. Lucifer felt this compulsion *before* sin was imposed on the planet and on the race.

Our hunger for more results from our status as the creature and not the Creator. We are finite and incomplete in comparison with the infinite, complete God who created us. We are always less and will always have less than God. Only God is the all-consuming, complete One in the universe. Thus we remain vulnerable to the allure of more. As such, God has created us in His image with the capacity to commune with and find our completeness in Him. He intended that He, the fully complete One, would be our all-sufficient source. He made us with an emptiness only He could fill. When we seek our significance outside of Him, whatever we strive for can never be enough.

We are built to find our significance in Him. There is no substitute. Hence the emptiness and sense of loss when our compulsion for more is directed not at more of Him but at more apart from Him.

CONTRIBUTION

Paul knew that one of the surest signs of freedom from the monster of more is the willingness to give, to let loose of what we have and invest it in the things of Christ that last forever. That's why Paul exhorted the wealthy people under Timothy's charge to "be generous and willing to share" (1 Timothy 6:8).

Paul's target audience was those on whom God has been pleased to bestow a measure of wealth. Paul addressed them in verse 17 as those who are "rich in this present world." We must be aware that many of God's people through diligent labor, sovereignly provided opportunities, good stewardship, and the gift of marketplace wisdom have been able to accumulate much of this world's goods. For people like this, the world has one basic message: guard what you have, salt it away, and multiply it. But God's principle is to "store up for yourselves treasures in heaven" (Matthew 6:20).

Having great power, possessions, or position is not in and of itself wrong. As we have discussed, having less may become wrong when those with little become proud of their lessness, as they remain closet coveters. It may be wrong to have more if we will become spiritually dysfunctional by not being content with what we have. As Paul said, there were times in his life when he had little and when he had much. Because of Christ, he was able to be content in either case.

If our spiritual target is contentment and character, the challenge for those whom God has blessed materially is to be committed to contribution. Paul warned them to avoid being conceited and succumbing to the temptation to trust in their wealth, "which is so uncertain" (1 Timothy 6:17). Rather, they are to place their trust in God who, interestingly, "richly provides us with everything for our enjoyment." Paul went on to say that they are to "do good, be rich in good deeds, and to be generous and willing to share" (v. 18). Of course, giving is to be part of our service to Christ regardless of the size of our bank accounts (1 Corinthians 16:2). Remember, Jesus affirmed and God multiplied the widow's mite.

REGAINING OUR BALANCE

Since the remedy to the madness for more is contentment, character, and contribution, we need to come to a biblical balance regarding gain. Contentment does not mean that we deny the stewardship of our gifts and capacities to succeed in the marketplace, or that we assign moral values to people's checking accounts. It means that we adopt the spirit of the famous naturalist John Muir, who once claimed he was richer than railroad magnate E. H. Harriman because "I have all the money I want and he hasn't." Muir knew contentment.

Scripture only speaks against a lack of contentment with what we have and a covetous spirit toward what others have. Is it wrong for career people to seek to do their best in the marketplace and in the process climb the corporate ladder with its rewards? If they are driven by gain, their endeavors are suspect. But if they are fulfilling their God-given drives and capacities, if they enjoy the fulfillment of work well done, then they may be blessed with more with which to contribute. They should also be free to enjoy what God has supplied without guilt and to do it all—to succeed to the maximum—for *His* glory and gain.

Our longing for more can't be obliterated, because we've been built for more—more in and through God. Francis Thompson's work, *The Hound of Heaven*, captures that truth as it describes his flight from God, who continued to patiently pursue him: "with unhurrying chase, and unperturbed pace / deliberate speed and majestic instancy . . ." Though he knew the one who followed loved him, he continued to flee, "lest having Him I must have naught beside."

But the hound of heaven continued to follow. Finally he heard a voice:

> *'Naught shelters thee who wilt not shelter me . . .*
> *Lo, all things fly thee when thou fliest me.*
> *. . .*
> *'Strange piteous, futile thing . . .*
> *Rise, clasp my hand, and come!*
> *. . .*
> *Ah, fondest, blindest, weakest,*
> *I am He whom thou seekest!'*[4]

When we find Him there is contentment, satisfaction, and true significance. The hymn writer Clara Task Williams celebrated the truth with this proclamation:

> *Hallelujah I have found Him*
> *Whom my soul so long has craved!*
> *Jesus satisfies my longing*
> *Through His blood I now am saved.*[5]

Yet, our fallenness has rendered us hopelessly and helplessly separated from Him and dead in our "trespasses and sins." It's no wonder, then, that mankind is driven compulsively to seek more where more is not. But this obsession can be cured. We can be gloriously liberated by redemption, the work of God through Christ that bridges the gap and restores our capacity to relate to and find satisfaction in God.

Redemption moves us from the random mode of living with its compulsion for more and its shame and loss to the redemptive mode of living. Here is fulfillment, found only in the gain and glory of

Christ. It begins with reunion. This is the only way to true significance and liberation!

> *None of us can deny our inner desire for more, and denial is not the answer. Like our drive for significance, and our need to fulfill our pleasure, pride, and passion, our desire for more is built into us by the Creator.*
>
> *We're built for fulfillment in the more of Christ, but our fallenness drives us to seek more in the things around us. Only when we come to Christ in repentance and faith can our God-given longing for more be truly satisfied.*

REFLECTIONS
ON REGRET

All of us wrestle with letting our significance rest solely in our relationship with Christ. Though He has brought us back to God through His saving sacrifice on the cross, often we think we need other ways to find significance in our lives. Reflect on the following questions regarding your source of significance and the threat of regrets in your life.

1. In what settings do you feel insignificant, and how do you react? How do you feel personally and biblically about your specific responses when your significance is threatened?

2. Specifically, how have your attempts to advance or protect your significance caused shame, loss, or regret?

   In the settings you identified above, what could you have done—or do now—to glorify Christ through your life and advance His cause?

3. Maybe you are tired of the competitiveness that the significance obsession imposes on friendships, relationships, and business associations. Would you be willing to take the steps necessary to make the transition from one who competes with others to one who complements and cooperates with others for God's glory?

4. In what ways is your life random?

   How would your friends answer that question for you? Your spouse? Your children? Your parents? Your colleagues at work?

   What random realities are there in your life that no one knows about?

   How would God answer that for you?

5. Who do you know who for the most part does not exhibit randomness in his or her life? How respected is this person by those who know him or her? What could you do to follow his or her pattern in your life?

6. Are you willing to live with what you have and where you are?

   Getting "more" sometimes means stepping across the line of love and loyalty to God. What entities on the other side of the line would be worth more to you than Christ? It's a matter of values—a matter of who or what is worth most to us.

   Are there some "more" kinds of things you are presently involved with that have lured you across the line? If so, honestly answer the following questions: What is her name (or his name)? What color is it? What brand is it?

   What can you do to turn your back on this person or object and return across the line to a loyal relationship with your Creator?

   What legitimate things has God given you to enjoy on His side of the line?

   Are you free to enjoy them . . . to enjoy them in grateful worship to our God who has provided them?

   How could you use them for His glory and gain?

PART TWO
REUNION

CHAPTER SIX

SIGNIFICANCE SECURED

In part one, we confronted the perilous results of seeking to fulfill our significance outside of God's plan. This pursuit can only produce regret because it is focused on things other than God, who made us for something more. The tragedy is that so many are searching for significance where it cannot be found, when our significance has already been secured for us in Christ.

Significance is not a search. It is a gift. When we receive full significance in Christ, we are liberated to live His significance through us and to enjoy His significant plans. This is our need. Only when we have been reunited with God through redemption will we discover the significance we were made to enjoy.

Remember Barbara, the young woman we met in chapter 1? She struggled with the haunting guilt and loss of worth that came from her attempts to find significance in attention from men, which she gained by using her sexuality. She felt significant in their attention but violated and shamed when they walked away.

It wasn't until Barbara realized that true significance was already hers in her relationship to God that things changed. She was liberated from her destructive obsession and was free to relate to men purely and constructively without shame and loss.

I also introduced you in chapter 1 to a pastor's wife of many years who told me how her heart had just been liberated from a negative, caustic, and resentful attitude toward the church where they served. She came to realize that the congregation's approval and appreciation were not the sources of her significance, but rather that it was in Christ.

This woman is representative of a whole legion of worthy though unaffirmed parents, housewives, laborers, teachers, helpers, and public servants who struggle with feelings of insignificance because they don't recognize what they possess already and who they are in Christ. His work on the cross has made us complete in Him, giving us many spiritual blessings and restoring us to our intended source of significance.

REDEMPTIVE RESTORATION

Redemption restores our potential to live the way we were built to live, finding our satisfaction and significance in a relationship with God through Jesus Christ. Our challenge is to get a grip on the results of redemption and live in the reality of all that it means. We too often settle for the "hell canceled, heaven guaranteed" aspect of redemption and never realize that it is more than a fire escape. Redemption was intended to revolutionize our lives, allowing us to live all of life transformed by the reality of our relationship with Christ.

TRANSFORMED RELATIONSHIPS

I will never forget the dramatic change that occurred in my life when I met my wife, Martie, in our freshman year of college. Feeling that someone that wonderful should not go unprotected, I asked if I could have the assignment. She agreed, and through our college years we developed a deepening love relationship that is now in its twenty-seventh year.

As I reflect back on my life before Martie and with Martie, I see the dramatic difference her presence has made. Life without her was focused primarily on me. It was often random and at times—too many times—irresponsible. But once she became a part of my life, I found that she occupied my thoughts and stretched my horizons. My deepening love for Martie meant that I not only lived *with* her, but *for* her. Significant relationships have a way of transforming us.

Those of us who are parents sometimes wonder if our kids will ever get a grip on life. Two of our children, Libby and Joe, are now married, and it has been interesting to watch the impact their relationship with their spouses has had on developing them. Most of what Martie and I weren't able to accomplish in our children's lives has been accomplished in their new relationships with other significant people, their spouses.

But it's not just the relationship. It's that the worth and value of the one they're related to, Libby's husband, Rod, and Joe's wife, Joy, impel them to responsible actions and reactions that enhance the dynamics of the relationship. That's how it is with you and me: Relationships with close friends bring unparalleled rewards into our lives.

Through the years I have had the opportunity to work with people who were struggling through different aspects of their relationships. Sometimes it was helping a marriage partner wake up to the reality and responsibilities of a spouse and children. The problem is that too many people want the joy of a relationship without the attendant responsibilities. Sadly, only later do they discover that, without doing their part, the expected joy does not follow.

I have a suspicion that for most of us the issue is not having a relationship with Christ, but waking up to its responsibilities and rewards. One of the great rewards of our redemption is that we no longer need to manufacture our own significance. It has been granted to us in Jesus Christ. What we need to do is wake up to the glorious reality of this truth and accept its privileged responsibility. When that happens, we are liberated to live for His significance and not our own.

Applying redemption to our struggle for significance liberates us from a whole litany of destructive behaviors and disappointing outcomes. For instance, gossip, slander, boasting, murmuring, and lying are no longer necessary to protect and enhance our significance. Manipulating and controlling people becomes unnecessary. Anger and bitterness can dissolve, and our pleasure, pride, and passion take on an entirely new meaning.

TRANSFORMED SIGNIFICANCE

As we have learned, in the random mode of living, we are constantly driven by external forces that allure our inner forces to do whatever it takes to gain significance. We have also seen, though, the result is not gain but loss and shame.

In the redemptive mode, on the other hand, we do not need to *seek* significance because it is already *secured* for us. This significance is not based on performance, power, prosperity, or position, but in the person of the living God releasing Christ within us. His internal presence and control give stability and certainty to our attitudes and actions as we surrender the controls to Him by yielding to His Lordship. Christ then transforms our passions into a passionate zeal for Him, the advance of His kingdom, and the good of others. As we are consumed with Him, our pride refocuses on Him, which produces an authentic humility that seeks to glorify God and not ourselves. And pleasure? Christ transforms it into a longing to please God and those whom God has trusted to our care.

The redemptive mode of living makes us people who are shaped and directed from the inside out, and we are thus free from the enslaving forces of the world around us. We are capable of controlling and using creation for the good of others and the glory of God, which is how He intended us to function. We are also stable and at peace, the restless and otherwise insatiable lust for significance fully satisfied.

What remains, then, is for us to understand the full impact of redemption as we learn to live in the redemptive mode.

REDEMPTIVE REUNION

Ever since Adam and Eve fell, all of us have been born in sin, separated from the God who is the only source and hope of true significance. Counselor Larry Crabb notes: "The human race got off on a seriously wrong foot when Eve yielded to Satan's lie that more satisfaction was available if she took matters into her own hands. When Adam joined her in looking for life outside of God's revealed will, he infected all his descendants with the disease of self-management."[1]

Realizing their shame and loss, Adam and Eve tried to cover their sin by sewing fig leaves together. Our world still specializes in fig leaves, because there is no hope of significance apart from God. When sin is present, as it is in all of us, there is also no hope of restoration to Him in and of ourselves and therefore no hope of true, shameless significance.

That is why redemption is such a pivotal and wonderful reality. The marvel of it all is that God has taken the initiative. He walked back into the Garden of Eden, now a fallen place, looking for Adam and Eve, the parents of what was now a fallen race. He could have annihilated the entire race in judgment for their rebellion against Him. Justice would have been well served. But in mercy and grace He sought them out. He called to Adam and Eve, drew them out of the bushes, and began a process of restoring them to Himself.

To restore them, God scrapped the fig leaves, which symbolized their shame and were only a cosmetic cover-up, and He covered our first parents with the skin of an animal sacrificed on their behalf (Genesis 3:21). It was a picture that would finally be fulfilled in the shed blood of Christ for our sins, which makes restoration with God possible and regains for us the settled and secure significance found only in Him.

Redemption through Christ is the only means of reconciliation with the Father. "I am the way and the truth and the life. No one comes to the Father except through me," Jesus said (John 14:6). He is the only solution to sin and our resulting alienation from God. And redemption renders us *complete* in Christ. Not perfect, but complete. No lack, nothing missing, no shortfall, no need to finish what is already completed. We are fully, completely restored to God.

As the apostle Paul told the Colossian church, "See to it that no one takes you captive through hollow and deceptive philosophy, which depends on human tradition and the basic principles of this world rather than on Christ. For in Christ all the fullness of the Deity lives in bodily form . . . " Paul concludes, "You have been given fullness in Christ, who is the head over every power and authority" (2:8–10).

This complete *redemptive reunion* of the creature with the Creator is secure. For those of us who are redeemed, the issue is no longer a search for significance by our own efforts, but the living out of a significance already secured in Him by His restoring love and mercy.

The foundation begins with our *reunion* to God. Being unalterably reconnected to the God of the universe, the only significant one, is the source of our significance. Such significance is not intrinsic to us; we have no real significance apart from Him. Our significance is found in Him alone and in the grace realities that God invests in us.

When we think of the things that bring us a sense of significance, we think of our worth, a positive identity, performance, prosperity, power, belonging, and position. All of these are fully provided in a relationship with God; they are ours through the finished work of Jesus Christ on the cross. When we understand all that we are in Him, searching for significance becomes unnecessary. Instead, we can rejoice in our secured significance in Him. Think of what we have in Christ because of the completed work of redemption!

WORTH

As Genesis 1:26 says, God's creative intent was to make us in His image, to create within us the capacity for a relationship with Him. But while all of us carry this image, we are hopelessly alienated from God by sin. At the moment of redemption, however, we are reunited with God and have the capacity to fulfill our role as image-bearers. There is no personal worth as deep and rich as the worth we have by being created in the image of God and reflecting His glory in our lives. In all creation, men and women alone have the privilege and dignity of being created in His image and, through redemption, being restored to the capacity of fulfilling their created destinies.

Redemption proves that we are desired by Him and loved by Him, so much that His Son died for us. For those of us who know Him, He has restored us to Him at a great price. Though unworthy, we have received worth through His love and grace.

IDENTITY

Significance also comes from our identity with Christ; significance and identity go hand in hand. Some time ago, my wife and I walked into a restaurant in Chicago with friends from out of town and saw wild-haired boxing promoter Don King sitting with the then-mayor of Chicago. Our friends didn't know either of the men, but when I pointed out that one had been Muhammad Ali's boxing promoter and the other was the mayor of Chicago, our friends were impressed. Both Don King and the mayor were significant because of who and what they were identified with.

Think of how often someone is introduced to you, or you are introduced to someone else, and the introduction is immediately followed by what you are identified with. "Hi. I want you to meet my friend Amanda. She's a doctor." Identity with that which is significant lends significance to us. Redemption has secured for us an identity as children of God; it doesn't get more significant than that.

How great is the love the Father has lavished on us, that we should be called children of God! And that is what we are! The reason the world does not know us is that it did not know him. Dear friends, now we are children of God, and what we will be has not yet been made known. But we know that when he appears, we shall be like him, for we shall see him as he is. (1 John 3:1–2)

As God's children, we are also citizens of His land (Philippians 3:20). The believers in Philippi would have appreciated this truth, because Philippi was a Roman colony whose people were Roman citizens. If you were a citizen of Rome during the height of the Roman Empire, your identity gave you great cultural and social significance. But the Philippian believers were citizens of an even greater place—heaven.

When I travel, I like to tell people that I live in Chicago. Chicago is a great city with great athletic teams, great cultural opportunities, a great location on Lake Michigan, some fine neighborhoods, and lots of good people. There is a sense of significance in being identified with the great city of Chicago. But this cannot compare with my identity as a child of the King of whose land I am a secure citizen.

PERFORMANCE AND AFFIRMATION

Redemption also means we are significant regardless of performance. While performance is important in the doing of good works and the faithful execution of our responsibilities, our significance in Christ is not secured by our efforts. It was secured by the stellar performance of Jesus Christ on the cross and through the empty tomb as He performed the work of redemption.

This truth releases me to perform on His behalf. Because my significance is fully secure, I am now able to serve for Christ's glory and the advance of His kingdom, which leads to His affirmation. We all need affirmation, but when we are secure in Christ we no longer need to live for human applause. Our pleasure comes from His commendation, "Well done, good and faithful servant."

Encouragement from others is important, but we are neither driven by it nor should we seek significance in it. If affirmation comes, it is merely frosting on our cake. There's a big difference between being encouraged by and driven by affirmation. We aren't driven by affirmation because we are significant in Christ and find our ultimate affirmation in Him.

PROSPERITY

In terms of prosperity, Scripture tells us that we are joint heirs with Jesus Christ (Romans 8:16–17). Those of us who have been reunited to God through Jesus Christ are rich in the things of the Spirit, have all of our needs met in Him, and have the promise of heaven.

As Paul said of Christ, "For you know the grace of our Lord Jesus Christ, that though he was rich, yet for your sakes he became poor, so that you through his poverty might become rich" (2 Corinthians 8:9).

I am reminded of the Puritan who was incarcerated for his faith in Christ. In his cramped jail cell he was fed one portion of bread and water each day. But the guard heard him exclaim one day as he prayed over his portion, "Thank you, Lord, for all of this and heaven too!" He recognized his blessings. Is there any earthly symbol of prosperity you would trade for the riches you have in Jesus Christ?

POWER

Redemption also secures for us the indwelling Holy Spirit, who empowers us with wisdom strong enough to confound our enemies and grace to strengthen us during every difficult time. We are empowered by the Word of God that directs us through every dark and treacherous path. Being released from our obsession with our significance, we are now free to use the Spirit's power to serve and empower others to the glory of God (Acts 1:8).

BELONGING

So much of our significance comes from what we belong to. I have friends who for personal and business reasons belong to some pretty nice clubs. It's interesting how these clubs become great measures of significance for some people. The smaller and less public the club, the more significance it offers its members.

If you are looking for something of significance to belong to, remember that there is nothing like the significance of being Christ's, belonging to His kingdom and His family with thousands of others who are redeemed. It would be a jaded and deluded view of life to believe that our significance comes from belonging to something earthbound and passing away, when by redemption we belong to the eternal God (Romans 8:16–17).

POSITION

And while many seek significance in the positions and titles they hold or seek to hold, whether it be president of the corporation or president of the club, we need to remember that we have a secured position in Christ as members of His kingdom. In that kingdom there are no superstars, just servants in His vast vineyard who are also ambassadors of the King. If you're interested in the significance of position, remember that "if we endure, we will also reign with Him" (2 Timothy 2:12). That's significance!

And although significance apart from God produces pride, our significance in God is a cause for genuine humility. This significance is ours not because we earned it or deserved it, but because of His unbelievably marvelous grace and His great love. As such we are humbly indebted to Him, happily for all eternity!

A PICTURE OF RESTORATION

Our trouble is that we so easily forget all that has been secured for us in redemption. For us to seek significance apart from Christ is like gilding the lily of His already completed work. Worse, it is an arrogant pursuit that distorts our testimony for Him. What a powerful opportunity we have to demonstrate to a watching world that Christ has liberated us from this clamoring, driving obsession to gain a significance that can never be found.

Perhaps the most graphic illustration Christ ever gave of restoration to significance is the story of the lost son and the forgiving father in Luke 15. You probably know the story. The younger son asks for his cut of the family inheritance to set off on an independent search for significance and fulfillment apart from his father.

SEPARATION FROM THE FATHER

The younger son already had more than enough to be content. His father's house contained plenty of servants and fatted calves to be had for grand celebrations. But in that culture, it was the oldest son who held the position of power and authority in the household, and who also received the majority of the inheritance. Though an heir of great wealth himself and of greater importance than all of the hired help, the younger son wanted more.

It may be that he knew he would never hold the significant place of head of the household. Obviously, he wanted significance on his own terms in a place where neither he nor his father were known. He reasoned that in the "distant country," he would have the chance to establish his own identity. And if it meant he would have to offend his father to find significance on his own terms, then so be it.

The offense to his father was very real. In that culture, to ask for your inheritance early meant that you wished your father was dead. In a patriarchal culture where the father was unconditionally respected, this was the worst thing a son could do to his father. His inheritance would be primarily land and flocks, which he cashed out. In Palestine, land is part of the family legacy. It is the deepest of offenses to sell family land. What the land produces and the flocks that feed there also comprised the "social security" income for aging parents. This son not only sold these off, but squandered them in a Gentile economy.

Just as sin always separates us from our father, so this son's offense demanded that he leave his hometown and a culture that would reject that kind of behavior. The offense in this story is not the "naughty" things he did in a foreign land, but the blatant and brutal disregard for his father and the significance he had as his father's son.

It should not go unnoticed that he sought pleasure for himself in another land, that his pride was offended by a social structure that elevated his older brother, and that his passions found playgrounds in a place outside the father's house.

So he crossed the line, as did Adam, Eve, Lucifer, and all the rest of us who found ourselves separated from real significance and searched for it where it cannot be found. The pattern of the prodigal's pilgrimage transcends time and culture and stands as a paradigm of the human dilemma apart from God.

SELF-INDULGENCE

The first phase is self-indulgence, in which we blissfully follow any and every star that offers to take us to significance and satisfaction. Scripture described the prodigal's search as "wild living" (v. 13), a life that is not secure or stable, but that randomly responds to seductions to our pleasure, pride, and passion.

SELF-EXPENSE

Self-indulgence inevitably leads to self-expense. The prodigal "spent everything" (v. 14). Indulgent lives spend relationships, health, wealth, self-worth, dignity, and a host of other valued resources. Sin is never an investment. It is always an expense. No wonder the prodigal "began to be in need."

SELF-DEGRADATION

Self-expense inevitably leads to self-degradation. He lands as a keeper of pigs, animals labeled as "unclean" in Jewish laws. Perhaps some passersby asked the youth, "What's a nice Jewish boy like you doing in a place like this?" He works for a Gentile pig farmer. He was so degraded that the food he had didn't begin to nourish or satisfy his daily needs.

SELF-REFORMATION

On that pig farm, he realized that his only hope was to be restored to his father's house. So he started the long trek home, determined to seek restoration. Interestingly, while he planned to recover his lost sense of significance by a renewed relationship with his father, he still wanted to retain a measure of independence from his father's authority. We see that in his plea to be made like one of the "hired men" (v. 19).

Hired men were day workers who took a wage and lived separately in the village. Bondservants were the most dedicated and dependent servants. Household servants were servants too, but held a measure of status in the home. The hired men were the most distant of the estate work force.

So the son wanted to be restored to his father, yet he wanted to be free to live as separately as possible. For this degraded seeker of significance, this was an attempt not at true repentance, but at self-reformation.

The plot turns dramatically when the father sees his son coming. Filled with compassion, the father runs to meet him and smothers him with kisses.

Frankly, I think this boy was stunned by his father's grace, because he said simply, "Father, I have sinned against heaven and against you.

I am no longer worthy to be called your son" (v. 21). Our best manuscripts do not include his request to be made a hired servant. Self-reformation fell by the road. This was simple, straightforward, non-negotiated, honest repentance. He recognized his sin and unworthiness before his father and threw himself on his father's mercy.

RESTORATION TO SONSHIP

Given the depth of the offense, it is amazing that his father fully restored him to sonship. For the prodigal, full significance was neither earned nor deserved. It was *secured* for him as a redemptive act of his father, who told the servants to bring him a robe, a sign of full sonship; a ring, a symbol of family authority; and sandals, a sign that he was a free man and not a slave. Then the fattened calf was slaughtered and a party thrown to mark the son's value and his inclusion in the family.

Remember that Christ told this story to explain why He was willing to spend time with "tax collectors and sinners" (v. 1). These were the two groups of people who were most distant and despised in Israel. Tax collectors had cast their lot with the occupying Roman forces by taking this "get-rich-quick" job while inflicting loss on their fellow Jews. Sinners were like the prodigal. They had decided to seek significance in their own way, living apart from the declared mandates of God.

Yet, Christ came to offer the gift of restoration through redemption and the secured significance of sonship, power, and freedom to any and all. To Pharisees, who mistakenly thought themselves significant, and to the worst, who had no sense of significance.

All of us who have come to Christ are reunited to God, who secures for us true worth, identity, affirmation, prosperity, power, and belonging. He is the only source of significance, and we are now free to live out His significance by glorifying Him in everything (1 Corinthians 10:31). As Paul declared, "I eagerly expect and hope that I will in no way be ashamed, but will have sufficient courage so that now as always Christ will be exalted in my body, whether by life or by death" (Philippians 1:20). He affirmed in Colossians 2:10 that we have been given "fullness in Christ." Christ has "rescued us from the dominion of darkness and brought us into the kingdom of the Son he loves, in whom we have redemption" (Colossians 1:13–14). Thus we are free to serve the One who is completely preeminent (vv. 15–18). When we are obsessed with our efforts to secure significance, we end up competing with Christ's preeminence instead of enabling His preeminence to be expressed through us.

SUBSTANTIAL HEALING

The late Francis Schaeffer called the experience of redemption a "substantial healing." There is a sense in which redemption, though fully accomplished, will not be fully experienced until we are in heaven. Redemption cancels the penalty of sin and restores us completely to God, and someday will free us from even the presence of sin. But until it is fully applied, we will struggle with the fallout of our inherent sinfulness: sickness, disappointment, temptation, seduction, sorrow, and even the residual of our struggle for significance apart from God. As Paul wrote:

> I consider that our present sufferings are not worth comparing with the glory that will be revealed in us. The creation waits in eager expectation for the sons of God to be revealed. For the creation was subjected to frustration, not by its own choice, but by the will of the one who subjected it, in hope that the creation itself will be liberated from its bondage to decay and brought into the glorious freedom of the children of God. We know that the whole creation has been groaning as in the pains of childbirth right up to the present time. Not only so, but we ourselves, who have the firstfruits of the Spirit, groan inwardly as we wait eagerly for our adoption as sons, the redemption of our bodies. For in this hope we were saved. But hope that is seen is no hope at all. Who hopes for what he already has? But if we hope for what we do not yet have, we wait for it patiently. (Romans 8:18–25)

What this means for those of us who are complete in God through Christ is that we should seek, with the Holy Spirit's help and the guidance of God's Word, to cultivate as full an experience of our redemption as possible. This process, called sanctification, means the development of God's thoughts, ways, attitudes, and intentions in our lives as we seek to become more like Him, less like our fallenness, and more useful in the advance of His kingdom. Colossians 3:1–17 speaks to this intentional, Spirit-empowered resolve in our lives.

SUBSTANTIAL GROWTH

The process of sanctification begins with the two basic objectives of redemption. The first is to be more committed to Christ's significance through me than to try and sew together the fig leaves of my own significance. The second objective of redemption is to live to advance His work and kingdom instead of my own agenda.

With these two redemptive objectives in mind, the first step in sanctification is a complete surrender to Christ and His will for us. This involves cultivating the *willingness* to sacrifice and the *commitment* to serve and if necessary suffer for the glory and gain of Christ.

We must also trust that in due time our affirmation will come from God. This confidence allows us to serve not to enhance our significance, but with a patience that waits for affirmation from Him. Peter assured us, "Humble yourselves, therefore, under God's mighty hand, that He may lift you up in due time" (1 Peter 5:6).

We will get to the specifics of sanctification in upcoming chapters. But let me underscore once again that it will be impossible to embrace God's plans for our lives if we are obsessed with our own significance, randomly acting out the whims and schemes of our instincts of pleasure, pride, and passion. It all begins with reinforcing the secured significance we already have in Christ. Let me suggest some important ways for us to do that.

First, we must be willing to celebrate and worship God for our full significance and completeness in Him, and commit ourselves to being satisfied with these. This will be challenging in a culture that offers material and emotional enticements as a source of significance apart from Him. This affirmation and celebration of our completeness will also be challenging because so many, even brothers and sisters in Christ, are swept away in their search for significance and may even for a while seem to gain from the experience. That's when we will need to remind ourselves again that any search for significance apart from Christ will end in loss and shame.

Second, we can reinforce the truth of our redemptive completeness by memorizing Scripture that underscores it, and by praying God's Word back to Him in worship in our devotions.

Third, we can pray regularly for God's guidance and insight into ways that we can more effectively magnify His significance and advance His kingdom. Prayer should also include repentance for specific acts of seeking to establish our own significance.

Fourth, we should target those situations in which we're most prone to slip back into the random mode of living. This means making plans to avoid these things, perhaps sharing our vulnerability with a person or group who can hold us accountable. As we reinforce our sense of significance in Christ, we will be able to surrender to His work in us and enjoy being a part of efforts to advance the significance of His work in this world.

> *Significance secured! That's a leading feature of the good news of our redemption. How liberating it is to be released from the futility of trying to sew together the fig leaves of significance apart from Christ.*
>
> *He has something so much better for us—restoration to the Father's house as full heirs. Everything we could wish for to complete our lives is available to us in Christ—including a sense of significance beyond anything this seductive world can offer.*

CHAPTER SEVEN

REDEMPTIVE RESTRUCTURING

"It's always worked for me before." How many times have you heard someone say that? Whether it's in business, at home, or in the culture at large, most people fall into familiar patterns or modes of behavior. The problem is things change, and the old ways don't always work.

Some businesses learn this lesson too late and lose out. Boarded-up factories all over the country prove this. Others change, retool, and grow. The same principle holds true in the spiritual realm. How much retooling do we need as people who have been redeemed from the old way of life? Let's see.

American business and industry have undergone a phenomenal, even radical change in the last two decades. For most of our history, America was the major industrial and economic power in the world and had the freedom to do almost what it pleased. But in the 1970s, a new world order began to emerge that forced American business to reevaluate, restructure, and respond to the rapidly changing environment or face loss and extinction. The world economy was becoming more interdependent, and high-tech industry began to dominate commerce. For perhaps the first time, the most valuable commodity on the market was not the goods and products we made with our hands, but information.

At the same time, Japan and Germany experienced a resurgence of their commercial base, bringing better-quality goods to our border than we were producing ourselves. Our skyrocketing costs of doing business were undercut by cheap labor in places like Mexico, China, Korea, and Taiwan. Burdensome bureaucratic and tax structures increased business overhead, and stymied efficiency and the capacity for quick and creative responses.

The mood of American business has also changed dramatically. It's doubtful whether any corporate CEO today could run a Fortune 500 company the way IBM founder Thomas Watson was said to have operated. According to a book by Watson's son, his office was connected to his father's office one floor above by a private staircase and a buzzer. All the senior Watson had to do was push the buzzer, and the junior Watson was obliged to hit the stairs right away, regardless of what he was doing. Any boss trying to do that today would probably be accused of harassment!

Many businesses have responded to the changes and are thriving in this new environment, while others flounder and fail. Those who have succeeded have planned to change and managed the change effectively.

This book is not about business, of course, but about the efficient, successful development of Christ's glory through us. It is about the gain of His kingdom, managed effectively through us. Yet, the parallels between business management and managing His glory through us are highly instructive.

Most of us who fail to be authentic, growing followers of Christ do so not because we don't have the ability, knowledge, help, resources, or interest. We have all of these in adequate measure. For most of us, the problem is the mismanagement of our resources and the assumption that we can live our new lives by the principles that worked for us in the old life. We continue to manage money, friends, adversaries, our sexuality, and our businesses by the ways of the fallen world from which we have been redeemed. Though our significance has been secured, we continue to live as though it has not, in bondage to the random whims of pleasure, pride, and passion.

Failure to live out our redemption through a restructured life— what I call redemptive restructuring—has greater consequences than the failure of a business. It puts families, churches, and the testimony of Christ at risk. It also leaves us empty at best, and victims of shame, loss, and regret at worst.

That's why it is vital that we not only revel in redemption, but pursue its full application so that God's redemptive purposes for us will be realized. This will bring great benefit to our Lord and His name, to those around us, and, yes, to our own sense of significance and well-being.

Before American industry restructured, managers had to analyze and understand the new economic realities. A clear understanding of the realities of redemption is vital to our growth as well. What, then, are these redemptive realities?

TWO WORLDS

To restructure our lives based on our redemption, we must realize that we live in two worlds. The first is the world that the New Testament calls the *cosmos*. This is the unredeemed world of humanity, ruled and manipulated by Satan for the advance of his destructive cause and the shaming and diminishing of the glory of our Creator. All of us, redeemed and unredeemed, live in this world. It has its own values, standards, expectations, and patterns of response. We were all born into this world and live as its citizens by its rules and regulations.

But at redemption, our citizenship was transferred to a completely different world with a distinct system of values, standards, expectations, and patterns of response. This is what the New Testament calls the *kingdom of Christ,* which Paul described in Colossians 1:13–14. We are now members of this kingdom, which is managed by Christ to advance the glory of God and to enrich eternity. And although we are still in the world, we are called to live according to the realities of Christ's kingdom.

Paul wrote, "Therefore, if anyone is in Christ, he is a new creation; the old has gone, the new has come!" (2 Corinthians 5:17). The apostle instructed us to surrender fully to God as an act of worship, and then outlined the process of transition from the old world order to the kingdom way of living: "Do not conform any longer to the pattern of this world, but be transformed by the renewing of your mind. Then you will be able to test and approve what God's will is—his good, pleasing and perfect will" (Romans 12:2).

In fact, the majority of the New Testament's exhortations deal with the importance of living accurately as kingdom citizens in this fallen, dark world. Scripture never allows us to live out our redemption by the rules of the old, soon-to-be-judged world order of Satan.

In John 17:15–17, Christ prayed not that His father would take us out of the world, but set us apart in the world by our commitment to the truth. Paul reminded us that we are citizens of heaven (Philippians 3:20). The use of the term *citizen* is intended to remind us that we live by the standards of the kingdom to which we belong, the kingdom of Christ, though we still live in the domain of darkness as "aliens and strangers." What else could we be in a world that is programmed to thwart God's purposes in our lives?

In calling us to live out our newness, Christ said, "No one sews a patch of unshrunk cloth on an old garment, for the patch will pull away from the garment, making the tear worse. Neither do men pour new wine into old wineskins. If they do, the skins will burst, the wine will run out and the wineskins will be ruined. No, they pour new wine into new wineskins, and both are preserved" (Matthew 9:16–17). He said this in response to a question by John the Baptist's disciples, who wondered why Christ's disciples did not fast like they did. In essence, Christ said that a new order had come, and that trying to live by the old ways in this new order would create major problems.

My generation saw an unforgettable example of this principle at work as we watched former prisoners of war return from Vietnam in the early 1970s. I'll never forget seeing these men step off the plane, some obviously crippled, all with weary, drawn faces, but smiling as they received the salutes of their comrades. Several of them stooped to kiss American soil, then came the happiest moment of all: the rush of waiting family members to embrace the prisoner and welcome him home.

As the POWs came home, heroic stories emerged of men who had held fast to their loyalty in the face of incredible suffering and pain. Some had become inspirational examples to their fellow prisoners, calling them to faithfulness whatever the cost. These men were in an alien, very hostile environment that called for new responses of courage and endurance many of the men never knew they were capable of. Trying to carry on in the old way, as if they had been back home, would have been disastrous. Our hostages in Lebanon have reported similar experiences as they endured years of captivity. We're not prisoners of war or hostages, but we're in a war!

Once we understand the reality of our new kingdom, to succeed in it we need to adopt the new objectives of kingdom living, new relationships, and new resolves to eliminate anything that impedes through us the kingdom goals—the glory and gain of Jesus Christ.

We must also learn to redirect our inner energies of pleasure, pride, and passion so that they become allies, not enemies, of authentic kingdom living. This radical restructuring of our lives is not incidental, but intentional. It's not automatic either, but comes through planned obedience.

TWO KINGDOM OBJECTIVES

American industry realized quickly that new objectives needed to be established in this new global environment. Instead of mere quantity, quality became the objective of corporate output. Instead of policies that served the company, it became necessary to make policies that served the consumer. Citizenship in Christ's kingdom also requires that we adopt two new objectives.

GOD'S GLORY

At the beginning of this book, I referred to the Westminster Shorter Catechism, which teaches that our chief purpose is to "glorify God and enjoy Him forever." Here is the first objective of kingdom living. Obviously, this cannot be lived out until we have secured our significance in Christ. Liberated from the obsession with our significance, we are now capable of dedicating all that we are and do to His glory.

Paul spelled out this objective clearly: "Do you not know that your body is a temple of the Holy Spirit, who is in you, whom you have received from God? You are not your own; you were bought at a price. Therefore honor God with your body" (1 Corinthians 6:19–20). As we saw earlier, the scope of the objective takes in every activity (1 Corinthians 10:31).

So pressing was this agenda for Paul that he declared it to be the objective of his life as he sat in a Roman prison waiting for Nero's decision on his life. "I eagerly expect and hope that I will in no way be ashamed, but will have sufficient courage so that now as always Christ will be exalted in my body, whether by life or by death. For to me, to live is Christ and to die is gain" (Philippians 1:20–21). The objective of Paul's life was Christ, and his gain awaited in the next world. Most of us live as though our gain is here and now as we gobble up every opportunity to gain advantage for ourselves. Not so! Kingdom objectives direct us to invest our lives in magnifying Christ in this world and experiencing our gain in the world to come.

When we have significance in Christ, we are secure and can step aside to let Him live through us. Two models who sought to advance God's glory and gain through Christ living within are John the Baptizer and the apostle Paul. Christ became preeminent in their lives, both in action and attitudes.

John the Baptizer gladly heralded the coming Christ even though the Gospels report that the baptizer was a stellar, well-known leader of his day. He had all the headlines! Crowds followed him. A household name, John was the center of many discussions among the intelligentsia and the religious leaders of his day. When Christ appeared, though, this high profile leader has an immediate response: "He must increase, but I must decrease"(NASB). John recognized the supremacy and priority of Jesus Christ; he was glad to humbly advance the significance of the Messiah.

The apostle Paul had the same response to the presence of Christ in his life. In Philippians 3 he presented a long list of credentials and accomplishments (vv. 5–6) that would impress all his readers. A "Hebrew of Hebrews," this Pharisee had established well his significance in religious circles. Yet Paul realized that all of this was worthless if he was to truly gain Christ. In the face of the supremacy of Christ, he regarded all things but "loss for the sake of Christ" (v. 7).

When Christ enters the arena of our lives, there need be no competition, for He has no peers. No one is even in second place. He is, and deserves to be, fully supreme. Therefore, magnifying Christ in our lives means a total, non-negotiated commitment to His significance.

Living to magnify Christ also means that we reflect His essential nature. Since He is truth, for example, we are truthful. His mercy, justice, compassion, righteousness, love, grace, and patience should be clearly evident in all we do. And as people note the unique difference, we readily give God the credit for what we have and have become in Him.

Ironically, some Christians, obsessed with their personal significance, when threatened will readily lie to maintain their worth; they will withhold love, mercy, and grace when it conflicts with their sense of significance. This is not kingdom living. To cross the line of righteousness to accumulate or guarantee our significance is never kingdom living. An obsession with personal significance will always be a competitor with Christ's significance through us. It is not until our significance compulsion is satisfied by our applying redemptive realities that we are free to magnify Him even at a loss to ourselves.

In a sense, magnifying the significance of Christ does involve a loss of independent identity. We are no longer self-made, self-managed people reflecting our glory, but rather "Christ-made" people reflecting His glory and gladly giving Him the credit. The song "My Tribute" has it right: "All that I am and ever hope to be, I owe it all to Thee."[1]

Maybe this example will help us understand what it means to glorify Christ. I recall being invited several years ago to a banquet, and as usual they invited my family to attend with me. We were seated on a raised dais, and I was placed next to the head of the whole affair. All of us had nametags. Martie was next to me, then came our daughter Libby, then our youngest son Matt next to her.

When we were finished eating, Matt (who was about eight at the time), walked over to me, tapped me on the shoulder, and asked if he could sit in my lap. Now you need to know that whenever the Stowell family goes to a restaurant, I often notice the server's nametag, call him or her by name, and strike up a conversation. So my children are used to noticing nametags. Sure enough, no sooner had Matthew landed in my lap than he turned his little head, read the nametag of the banquet leader next to me, and said, "Hi, John. How are you tonight?"

Matthew is a chip off the old block. And, in essence, his imitation of me glorified his father. Granted, it's not much glory. But the principle is that when we reflect the qualities and characteristics of our heavenly Father, we bring Him glory. In a very real sense, we are chips off the divine block. We are not divine, of course. But redemption has rekindled within us the capacity to reflect His image, so that the love, mercy, grace, justice, righteousness, and wisdom of the invisible God might become visible through us. Then God will become credible to a world that considers Him incredible. This is our redemptive privilege.

I was shown a wonderful example of this on another occasion by my Hebrew professor in seminary, when he received too much change at the bank. He turned back and said to the teller, "I'm sorry, but you've given me too much."

She said, "My, you're an honest man."

"It's not that I'm an honest man," he answered. "It's that Jesus Christ has changed my life."

How beautiful was that simple act of worship. He gave credit to God and expressed what He was worth.

The psalmist was driven by this agenda as he asked for God's blessing:

> May God be gracious to us and bless us and make his face shine upon us; may your ways be known on earth, your salvation among all nations. May the peoples praise you, O God; may all the peoples praise you. May the nations be glad and sing for joy, for you rule the peoples justly and guide the nations of the earth. May the peoples praise you, O God; may all the peoples praise you. Then the land will yield its harvest, and God, our God, will bless us. God will bless us, and all the ends of the earth will fear him. (Psalm 67:1–7)

What a dramatically different perspective. The psalmist sought the blessing of God on his life not to consume it on himself, but so that people would come to know what God is like and be compelled to praise Him and fear His name.

God's objective for all of creation is to witness to the reality of His character and perfection. As Psalm 19:1 proclaims, "The heavens declare the glory of God." Our commitment to glorify God, made possible by our redemptive reunion with the true source of significance, puts us in line with His intended purpose and pleasure for our lives.

CHRIST'S KINGDOM

The second objective of Christ's new order is to dedicate ourselves to the advance of His kingdom. We must, of course, believe that the kingdom itself has significance and is worth our time. Christ's directive to "seek first his kingdom" (Matthew 6:33) outlines the objective clearly. When we are consumed with the duties and anxieties of life in the cosmos, the old world order, we are distracted from effective service in the kingdom of Christ. Christ assures us that the Father knows our needs. As we make the kingdom a priority, He will meet our earthly needs. This is not a call to abandon our daily responsibilities.

But when distraction and anxiety seduce us to deny our kingdom responsibilities, our commitment must be to the kingdom, trusting God to meet our temporal needs.

What comprises this kingdom to which we are to commit ourselves? It is not the stuff of our kingdoms: castles, cars, clout, and currency. Rather, it is a kingdom whose values are anchored in eternity. In fact, the pivotal reality of Christ's kingdom is eternity. As the eternal King, Christ eclipses any temporal authority in our lives. People become our highest priority because only people are eternal. Their eternal destiny is the driving issue in Christ's kingdom.

Since it is His kingdom, it is managed by His eternal values that elevate giving over getting, serving over being served, people over things, love over self, forgiveness over hate, and meekness over revenge. Eternal values mean we will value responsibility over pleasure, suffering and sacrifice over comfort and convenience, justice and fairness over self-serving advance, family over career, compassion over apathy, and godliness over gain.

Kingdom people are not shaken by threats from this present world. They have cast their lot with a far more significant endeavor. They live by kingdom rather than cosmos values, and will suffer and die for their King if necessary.

By now it should be obvious that an obsession with our significance hinders the advance of Christ's significant kingdom through us. For most people, values like serving, giving, forgiving, sacrifice, and suffering threaten the attempts to build significance through personal kingdoms.

Instead, recognizing that our significance has been secured in Christ, Christians should be free to advance the kingdom of their dear Lord, even if it means temporary loss or the surrender of their personal kingdoms.

It is only when we undergo redemptive restructuring that we are released to achieve redemption's two objectives: an unwavering commitment to magnifying Christ, and living to advance His kingdom.

NEW MANAGEMENT

Redemptive restructuring requires not only restructuring our objectives to seek the glory and gain of Christ, but it also demands that we submit ourselves to new control in the bunkers of our souls. Until we do so, we remain supreme commander—seeking significance through the exercise of our pleasure, pride, and passion. Why do we need new management? Because these random responses often became ingrained habit patterns that required little thought on our part.

In the restructuring of our lives Christ heads the management team. Left to ourselves, we fallen and finite beings will be quickly tossed around by the winds of the powerful influences in our environment. Christ, on the other hand, is wise, infinite, all-powerful, and changeless, the embodiment of love, justice, mercy, and righteousness. He is God, and He will manage our lives in ways that produce His character through us.

At redemption, Christ came to dwell within us in the person of the Holy Spirit. The Spirit's indwelling presence is not just for our comfort and pleasure, but for our guidance that we might live as kingdom people. Christ clearly outlined the ministry of the Spirit as He prepared His disciples for life without His physical presence: "I will ask the Father, and he will give you another Counselor to be with you forever—the Spirit of truth. The world cannot accept him, because it neither sees him nor knows him. But you know him, for he lives with you and will be in you" (John 14:16–17).

Later Christ returned to the issue of the Holy Spirit, describing His role in our lives:

> I tell you the truth: It is for your good that I am going away. Unless I go away, the Counselor will not come to you; but if I go, I will send him to you. When he comes, he will convict the world of guilt in regard to sin and righteousness and judgment: in regard to sin, because men do not believe in me; in regard to righteousness, because I am going to the Father, where you can see me no longer; and in regard to judgment, because the prince of this world now stands condemned. I have much more to say to you, more than you can now bear. But when he, the Spirit of truth, comes, he will guide you into all truth. He will not speak on his own; he will speak only what he hears, and he will tell you what is yet to come. He will bring glory to me by taking from what is mine and making it known to you. (John 16:7–14)

Notice the function of the indwelling Spirit is to magnify and glorify Christ, not our own significance. The new management has a completely new goal in mind. Note too that the Spirit comes to guide us into *all* truth: not just cognitive truth, but also experiential, practical truth that we can live out every day.

Not only does the Spirit of Christ rule within because it is His intended purpose. It is also His rightful place since He too is God. Who among the redeemed would not believe that the God of the universe had the right to be the directing force of their lives?

As Americans, we are fortunate to be living in a democracy. Yet living in our democracy limits our understanding of the Lordship of Christ. We elect our leaders, who serve at the pleasure of the people. They do not serve by right, but by permission. It is easy, then, for us to look at the Lordship of Christ as something of a permission we grant Him, to be reclaimed when we want to govern our lives, even temporarily. But we do not make Jesus Lord. He *is* Lord! (Philippians 2:11). As such, He has the right to call the shots in our lives toward His glory and the advance of His kingdom. He will manage every aspect of our lives toward the objectives of the kingdom.

And since I no longer need to be obsessed with my significance, I can dedicate my heart, will, emotions, dreams, and desires to the One who does all things well and works all things together for my good. The key to the restructured life is Christ, through the person of the Holy Spirit, leading the management team in the core of my being.

NEW DIRECTION

Perhaps the most fulfilling aspect of our redemptive restructuring is that we escape being victimized by the external seductions of the world. Because the new management in our lives controls us from within, we become inner-directed people who can initiate the wisdom, truth, and grace of Christ in every effort and relationship.

Paul called this becoming mature in Christ, a process that is at work in us,

> until we all reach unity in the faith and in the knowledge of the Son of God and become mature, attaining to the whole measure of the fullness of Christ. Then we will no longer be infants, tossed back and forth by the waves, and blown here and there by every wind of teaching and by the cunning and craftiness of men in their deceitful scheming. Instead, speaking the truth in love, we will in all things grow up into him who is the Head, that is, Christ. (Ephesians 4:13–15)

Later, the apostle gave us this call to inner-directed living:

Be very careful, then, how you live—not as unwise but as wise, making the most of every opportunity, because the days are evil. Therefore do not be foolish, but understand what the Lord's will is. Do not get drunk on wine, which leads to debauchery. Instead, be filled with the Spirit (Ephesians 5:15–18).

I love the sense of stability, strength, and confidence that comes from Christ reigning in my heart, directing me to fulfill His redemptive objectives. To be free from the seductive energies in my world that victimize me, whiplash my life, and engender shame and loss is a redemptive privilege of unparalleled worth.

NEW DEFINITION

Another of the Holy Spirit's redemptive works is to redirect our energies of pleasure, pride, and passion toward glorifying God and advancing His kingdom. If these energies are not redirected, they will derail our redemptive restructuring by seducing us to cross the line of love and loyalty to God.

The Spirit redefines these energies and redirects their influence and power toward productive, satisfying results. Redemption was not intended to leave us void of pleasure, pride, or passion. Quite the opposite. These energies need only to be refocused and restored to their intended function.

In fact, these forces are so critical to the process I've been describing that we need to understand how they make the transition from their old form to their redeemed form.

> *One of the fundamental truths about us as redeemed people is that we are totally new persons in Christ. Since that's true, it's impossible for us to live as if nothing has changed, to continue in our old ways of responding and expect them to move us toward maturity in Christ. New objectives require new direction and management.*

REFLECTIONS
ON REUNION

1. In what ways would life be different for you if your search for significance were ended and you focused your mind and heart on the truth that God alone is the source of significance? Remember that your significance is fully secured regardless of who you are or what you have or have not done.

   How would your relationships, self-perception, worship, and obedience be affected?

2. Have you ever thought of your life as being helplessly separated from God by sin? Of having no significance apart from Him? Of having deeply offended Him by the very nature of our existence?

   Have you ever thought of reaching out to Him in repentance for reunion through the completed work of Christ for you? What do you think is keeping you from accepting His restoring offer of love and grace? Is it worth it?

3. If you are a Christian, do you still search for significance apart from God? What is it you are still looking for, seeing that you have Him? Recall this truth from Part 2: In Him we have all the attendant benefits of worth, identity, performance, affirmation, prosperity, power, belonging, and position.

   What could you do to rivet the reality of a significance secured in your heart and mind so that you are not seduced across the line to the mirage of more—which in reality is always less?

4. Are you willing to accept the fact that all of us who have been re-demptively restored to God have been fully restored without quali-fication, probation, or performance?

   Like the Prodigal Son, we are fully accepted as sons and daugh-ters with all the intended rights and privileges. Think through the list of redemptive privileges that are secured for you, and secure your sense of significance by reflecting on what they mean to you in practical, day-to-day terms.

5. If someone casually asked, "What is your purpose in life?" how would you answer? Would you say "the glory and gain of Christ in me and through me"? If not, why not?

   A restructured life lives to glorify and advance the cause of Christ. Reflect specifically on ways you could express this redemp-tive calling—at home, in the marketplace, at church, in leisure, and in friendships.

6. Are you still in the process of restructuring your life for His glory and gain? You're not alone. Why not get together with two or three trusted friends in Christ and plan to encourage and hold one an-other accountable. Together you can work for growth in advancing the glory and gain of Christ in all aspects of your lives.

PART THREE
REFOCUS

CHAPTER EIGHT

THE PLEASURE PURSUIT

God's redemptive purpose for us was far more than canceling hell and guaranteeing heaven. He intended redemption to be a total refocus of our lives from the inside out. Redemption is the act of God liberating me from the ravages of sin and creating a completely new me.

As a redeemed person, the life I now have will reach ultimate perfection in heaven. In the meantime, redemption works to refocus my mind and heart on God's redemptive purpose for my life—to reflect His glory and to live for his gain. This requires a retooling of my three primary energies of pleasure, pride, and passion. Let's begin by seeing what a refocused pleasure looks like.

Liberated! Through our restoration to Christ, who has secured for us full significance through His sacrifice on the cross, our obsession with our own significance is banished from our lives.

Yet like bandits hiding in the rocks, the surging energies within wait to ambush our liberation celebration. If not refocused toward God's redemptive plans, the forces of pleasure, pride, and passion can sabotage almost at will Christ's glory and gain through us.

For instance, we may seek to advance Christ's kingdom by sacrificial giving to His work, only to have pride step in, take the credit, and hurl us back into the significance syndrome. Or we might seek to serve Christ with our lives, only to have the passion for power and position twist our perspective, like the disciples who constantly debated about which of them would be the greatest in the kingdom. Or our pleasure instinct might derail our redemptive pursuits by using "wine, women, and song" to abort the growth and glory of Christ in our lives.

Our redemptive restructuring isn't complete until we deal with the trigger-happy instincts of pleasure, pride, and passion. The goal is not their eradication. God is not interested in pleasureless, prideless, passionless Christians. In fact, we have seen that these instincts are created within us. It would be impossible to eliminate them, and frustrating, to say the least, to try and suppress them.

We have fostered an attitude in the body of Christ that inflicts unwarranted guilt if we seem to have too much pleasure, too much pride, too much passion. We have sanctified a sense of stoical sobriety, doormat humility, and placid emotions that has neutralized our impact and made our distorted Christianity look unappealing to the world around us. We're like the man on a bus who was extremely somber and sad-faced; we confuse those who watch us.

After watching the sad-faced man board the bus like this for several days, a curious fellow rider asked him, "Excuse me, but are you a minister?"

"No," the man replied. "I just haven't been feeling well lately."

Strangely, some believers take pleasure in their pleasurelessness, pride in their humility, and become suspiciously passionate about the loose passions in our culture. They also become critical of others who worship Christ with passion and enthusiasm. And on occasion, they even try to squeeze God into this mold. C. S. Lewis told about the schoolboy who was asked what he thought God was like. He replied that as far as he could make out, God was "the sort of person who is always snooping round to see if anyone is enjoying himself and then trying to stop it."[1]

It is not the eradication, suppression, or theological flogging of these inner energies that is required of us. What is needed is their radical redefinition, redirection, and diligent management to unleash their power in the advance of Christ's kingdom. They will either compete with and defeat this pursuit, or they will become our allies to aid and empower the glory and gain of Christ through us.

Given the crucial importance of refocusing these energies that threaten our liberation, we must look at each one from the perspective of its true, God-given purpose. We begin with pleasure.

PLEASURE PURSUED

Every schoolchild knows that the Declaration of Independence grants us "the pursuit of happiness" as an inalienable right. Yet pleasure was never intended to be a goal that we strive for, but a by-product of living in obedience to God and serving others. Let's take a look at pleasure as it really is and as it is intended to function.

The Greek word for pleasure is the word we translate as *hedonism*. Hedonism is living with a focus on pleasure, the "I'll do whatever pleases me and makes me happy" way of life. When hedonism becomes a compelling drive, we are immediately vulnerable to a hoard of seductions, beginning with pleasure. From the allure of an affair to pornography, or any other pleasure offered us, we will invent ways to consume the fruit that the adversary offers. Hedonists have been around forever, but it was in my generation that Hugh Hefner codified hedonism into the "Playboy Philosophy." Hefner's basic premise is simple. "We reject any philosophy which holds that a man must deny himself for others."[2]

Granted, pleasure is real, fulfilling, and satisfying. But when it is pursued apart from and in disobedience to God, it is *seasonal* and ultimately *sorrowful*. Moses recognized this and so chose to suffer affliction with the people of God "rather than enjoy the pleasures of sin for a short time" (Hebrews 11:25). Let's face it, sin would have no appeal if there were no pleasure offered as bait.

How boring it would be to cheat in business if there were not the pleasure of pounding your competitor one more time, or the pleasure of watching your bank account grow. If sin had no attendant pleasure kick, if it were neutral or even painful, it could be seen for its true ugliness, and there would be a lot fewer takers. But sin *is* pleasurable . . . for "a short time." It even offers satisfaction . . . for a short time. When the pleasure expires—and it always does—we are left with the sorrow, shame, and loss that sin always brings. This may be part of what Proverbs 21:17 means when it warns, "He who loves pleasure will become poor."

MISDIRECTED PLEASURE

The example of Moses' life in Egypt puts this reality in bold relief. His position as the son of Pharaoh's daughter put the expansive pleasures of a wildly sensuous and sophisticated culture at his fingertips. Yet he refused the seasonal pleasures of sin, choosing instead a future reward at the hand of his God. For Moses it was a choice between short-term gain and long-term loss, or short-term loss and long-term gain.

The Prodigal Son "squandered his wealth in wild living," and soon "he began to be in need" (Luke 15:14). The pleasures of the distant country not only seduced him, but consumed him and left him destitute. Godless pleasure is the lure to ultimate loss.

The love of pleasure sets us in opposition to love for God. Paul left no doubt about that. The end times, he said, will be marked by people who are "lovers of pleasure rather than lovers of God" (2 Timothy 3:2–4). Life often brings us to a crossroad where we are given the choice to seek immediate pleasure or to obey God.

The choice is brutally clear and those who are addicted to pleasure, who live to pursue it, will love their pleasure more than they love God. If an unwanted child threatens the mother's happiness, then abortion is the choice to preserve the mother's long-term pleasure. If a dating relationship seems to assure pleasure, yet it is an unequal yoke with a non-Christian that debilitates our walk with God, a pleasure-lover will choose the relationship over the will of God.

It's an interesting comment on our values that when push comes to shove, we readily opt for short-term pleasure over our allegiance to Him who loves us and gave Himself for us. In reality, our pleasure impulse, defiled by our fallenness, competes with God's glory and His gain.

The pursuit of pleasure can distract us from the life-changing impact of God's Word. A person can sit in church under the conviction of the Word as its truth pierces his or her soul, only to have its power eclipsed by the pleasurable thrill of a sexual affair or a shady business deal. Or the person may hear none of the message, since he's concentrating on that 2:42 tee time or she's thinking how pleased her husband will be that she's finally perfected his favorite dessert, or perhaps their thoughts are on the new car being delivered on Monday morning. And once more the probing, transforming power of the Word is buried under the rubble of temporary pleasure. Instead, a person must realize that the truth of the Scripture may demand denying himself some fleeting thrill. Christ warned that the seed of the Word sometimes falls among the thorns, landing on "those who hear, but as they go on their way they are choked by worries, riches and pleasure, and they do not mature" (Luke 8:14).

The pursuit of pleasure may destroy relationships. James asked, "What causes fights and quarrels among you? Don't they come from your desires that battle within you?" (James 4:1). Pleasure agendas often clash when two pleasure-seekers seek to build a relationship. The pleasure of power and position can only be consumed by one person at a time, and usually at someone else's expense. "I want to play tennis" clashes with "I want to talk with you." "I want to be free" clashes with "I want the pleasure of your company."

The pursuit of pleasure distorts and dulls our prayer life. James went on to say, "When you ask, you do not receive, because you ask with wrong motives, that you may spend what you get on your pleasures" (4:3). While this is true in terms of much of what we ask for, it is especially true of the heretical "health, wealth, and happiness" gospel we talked about earlier. Prayer is not a manipulative weapon to force God to grant us pleasure. It is a means by which we worship Him, finding peace in the midst of pain and grace and mercy to help in the time of need.

The pursuit of pleasure also leaves us empty. In Ecclesiastes 2, Solomon verified the hollowness of pleasure-seeking as he related his pleasure pursuit: "I thought in my heart, 'Come now, I will test you with pleasure to find out what is good.' But that also proved to be meaningless. 'Laughter,' I said, 'is foolish. And what does pleasure accomplish?'" (vv. 1–2).

This great king went on to explain how he tested the pleasures of wine, great accomplishments in the workplace, gardens, slaves, and large portfolios of herds, flocks, silver, and gold. He enjoyed the pleasures of the women in his harem and denied himself nothing that he desired. Yet, he found it all to be empty (v. 11). What a commentary on the futility of plenty without meaning.

Finally, *the pursuit of pleasure can be eternally fatal* apart from God. Pleasure often clouds the reality of heaven and hell. This is what happened to the rich but foolish farmer of Luke 12. He was merry with much—perhaps he thought he had everything—yet God called him a fool for not having prepared for eternity.

THE INSIGNIFICANCE OF MOMENTARY PLEASURE

The message of our culture is loud and clear. The more capacity you have to indulge in pleasure, the more significant you are. Who are the significant among us? Those who go on exotic vacations, throw lavish parties, whose fame lures the "beautiful people" to their side, whose fantasies are fulfilled, and who have the time to frolic on the exotic and erotic playgrounds of life.

Yet, the Scripture snaps us back to the reality that pleasure outside of its intended sphere is a short trip with a destination of shame, loss, and regret. To be enticed by the pleasures of the world is to be vulnerable to a broad array of sins, and at best to keep the only source of significance at arm's length. Pleasure-seekers incapacitate themselves when it comes to fulfilling the redemptive pursuits of God's glory and gain, as their lives are consumed with the glory and gain of personal pleasure. As such, pleasure becomes the manipulating manager of our lives.

It's no wonder that historically the redeemed community has looked askance at pleasure. Often, though, we have tipped the scales the other way. And while some may admit that we ought to have fun, the impression is left that there should not be too much of it.

In kindergarten my favorite time was recess. Even back then they knew that children needed a break from the stress of academic pursuits to enjoy life. We never outgrow our need for recess. And those who refuse to take it biblically will find that Satan builds his own playground for them. In fact, as we shall see, a true understanding of redemptive pleasure makes it an untainted experience that plays a legitimate role in life. Such pleasure becomes an ally in God's redemptive purpose.

THE GOD OF PLEASURE

Among their many gods the Greeks included Dionysus, the god of pleasure. He was one of a whole array of pagan personalities that competed for place and influence in Greek society with Zeus, the god of power, Aphrodite, the goddess of love, and others who clamored for cultural clout. People who worshiped at the temple of Dionysus reveled in orgies of sex, wine, and wanton pleasure only to find that their reward was measured in disease, illegitimate children, jealousies, and revenge.

When we think of the one true God, we realize that He is not a group of independent deities vying for power and position. His attributes do not compete, but blend into a magnificent composite of unsurpassed fullness and perfection. To delete, discount, or depreciate any aspect of His divine existence skews not only our knowledge of Him, but our view of life as well. We readily recognize that He is a God of power, love, justice, mercy, grace, righteousness, and a host of other attributes. But my guess is that most of us—maybe all of us—would be reluctant to say that He is the God of pleasure. But He is.

Pleasure is intrinsic to God's being. He both experiences pleasure and provides pleasure to those whom He has created. And being made in His image, the experience of pleasure is not only possible for us, but a legitimate reality as we live out His fullness. Understanding a restructured, redemptive sense of pleasure begins by affirming God's experience of pleasure. Scripture is replete with references to it.

For instance, God finds pleasure in the work of His hands. Genesis records that He looked at what He had made and pronounced it good. Revelation 4:11 says that God created all things at the pleasure of His will. The King James Version translates the final phrase of this verse, "and for thy pleasure they were created."

The highlight of God's pleasure is in the climax of His created work: mankind. According to Psalm 149:4, "The Lord takes delight in his people." He enjoys it when His people prosper (Psalm 35:27), when they praise Him and are grateful (Hebrew 13:15), when they are hospitable and do good (Hebrew 13:16). He is pleased—in fact, it is a "fragrant offering" to Him—when we give sacrificially to advance His cause (Philippians 4:18) and when an upright person prays (Proverbs 15:8–9). He finds pleasure in those who do His will and His work (Philippians 2:13).

These pleasure points make it clear that the primary source of God's pleasure is in relationships with redeemed people who live according to His created purpose. Conversely, Scripture teaches that He has no pleasure in fools (Ecclesiastes 5:4) and no pleasure in wickedness (Psalm 5:4). Nor does He take pleasure in those who rely on physical strength instead of His faithful love (Psalm 147:10–11).

THE PEOPLE OF HIS PLEASURE

Not only do we bring God pleasure, but He bestows His pleasure on us. There is an intrinsic desire in us to please others, especially our parents, and to feel the pleasure of their acceptance. To this day I desire to please my parents, and I can see the ways my children strive to please Martie and me. So deeply implanted is this desire that some people become performance-driven people pleasers because they never enjoyed their parents' pleasure and approval. In fact, the desire to be a pleasure to others, and to be affirmed in the process, drives some people to sexual, ethical, and moral downfalls because they long to know the pleasure of another person's approval.

This pattern is pervasive because God built us to find pleasure in pleasing Him and being affirmed by Him. God created Eden as an environment in which pleasure could be shared, and created Adam and Eve in His image so that they could *enjoy* a relationship with Him. Pleasing God meant being stewards of their surroundings, obeying Him by not eating of the forbidden fruit, and knowing the pleasure of His fellowship.

LIVING TO PLEASE GOD

So much of our perception of Christianity is upside down. We wonder if we can trust God when the real issue is, "Can He trust me?" We wonder if He loves us. Of course He does—He is love, and He extends love to us unconditionally. The right question is, "Do I love Him?" We wonder whether He will be faithful to us. Our concern should be, "Will we be faithful to Him?" And so it is with pleasure. We wonder if God will make us happy—will He bring pleasure to us—when the more pressing question is, "Will I bring pleasure to Him?"

It's clear from the New Testament that redemptive restructuring restores our pleasure to its proper focus: to please God and know the pleasure of His affirmation. This accomplishes two things. First, it defines pleasure not as a pursuit apart from God, but as a by-product of faithfulness to God. Second, a focus on finding pleasure in God and His purposes makes pleasure a supporting energy as we live out God's redemptive purposes. Pleasure no longer competes with our freedom from our significance obsession, but actually supports us in this freedom.

That this is the redemptive focus is supported by New Testament passages which underscore the process. Christ, who came to show us the pattern of redemptive living, said of His life, "I seek not to please myself but him who sent me" (John 5:30). The example of Christ is that we live to please our heavenly Father and others around us who are in need. "We who are strong ought to bear with the failings of the weak and not to please ourselves. Each of us should please his neighbor for his good, to build him up. For even Christ did not please himself . . . " (Romans 15:1–3).

Paul also said that we are "to please him in every way" (Colossians 1:10) and "make it our goal to please him" (2 Corinthians 5:9).

As we conform to our Father's righteous expectations, Scripture promises us two by-products of living to please God: happiness and joy (Psalm 1:1–3). Verses 4–5 offer an interesting and sobering contrast, those who have sought life on their own terms. In James 5:1–5, the apostle alluded to the end of those who live for their pleasure apart from God:

> Now listen, you rich people, weep and wail because of the misery that is coming upon you. Your wealth has rotted, and moths have eaten your clothes. Your gold and silver are corroded. Their corrosion will testify against you and eat your flesh like fire. You have hoarded wealth in the last days. Look! The wages you failed to pay the workmen who mowed your fields are crying out against you. The cries of the harvesters have reached the ears of the Lord Almighty. You have lived on earth in luxury and self-indulgence. You have fattened yourselves in the day of slaughter.

This contrast is also driven home in Galatians 5, where Paul describes a life apart from the Spirit of God as yielding "sexual immorality, impurity and debauchery; idolatry and witchcraft; hatred, discord, jealousy, fits of rage, selfish ambition, dissensions, factions and envy; drunkenness, orgies, and the like. I warn you, as I did before, that those who live like this will not inherit the kingdom of God" (vv. 19–21). The life that conforms to the Spirit, however, knows the pleasurable results of producing the fruit of the Spirit (vv. 22–23).

The themes of happiness and joy as outgrowths of a faithful, obedient life are underscored in Christ's words to His disciples in John

15:9–11: "As the Father has loved me, so have I loved you. Now remain in my love. If you obey my commands, you will remain in my love, just as I have obeyed my Father's commands and remain in his love. I have told you this so that my joy may be in you and your joy may be complete." In fact, the psalmist declares that God desires to bestow pleasure on His own. Psalm 16:11 says, "You have made known to me the path of life; you will fill me with joy in your presence, with eternal pleasures at your right hand," and in Psalm 36:8, David says of God's faithfulness to men, "They feast on the abundance of your house; you give them drink from your river of delights."

The pleasure that is a by-product of living to please God is not simply a package of thrills. It is rather, according to the Hebrew of Psalm 1:1, the pleasure of a life that is "straight" or "correct." Not straight in the sense of strict or stoic, but clean, without pretense or hypocrisy, free from the clutter of shame, loss, and regret. Satan appeals to our pleasure instinct with momentary "highs" that are fraught with devastating downsides. True pleasure is experienced in the deep, settled rightness of a life committed to God's glory and gain. When we experience life at its high points, by serving God freely, we can laugh with depth and unhindered appreciation.

"God values pleasure, both his and ours, and it is his pleasure to give us pleasure as a fruit of his saving love," writes J. I. Packer.[3]

Living to please God has many other positive by-products. It makes our relationships more fulfilling as we relate to others not for what they give us, but for what we can contribute to their pleasure.

THE PLEASURE OF SERVING OTHERS

My former seminary professor and mentor, Dr. Howard Hendricks, tells the story of being on an airplane that sat on the hot tarmac of the Dallas-Ft. Worth Airport one day for more than three hours. As the temperature inside the plane heated up, so did the passengers. Dr. Hendricks says he was particularly impressed with one flight attendant, who fielded the complaints, angry looks, and barbed comments with unusual calmness and grace.

Later, as he left the plane he introduced himself and said, "May I have your name? I want to write a note to your boss at American Airlines, commending your great service and attitude."

"That's kind of you," she replied. "I appreciate it. But I don't really work for American Airlines. I'm serving the Lord."

That flight attendant must have known Colossians 3:22–24, where Paul told employees:

> Obey your earthly masters in everything; and do it, not only when their eye is on you and to win their favor, but with sincerity of heart and reverence for the Lord. Whatever you do, work at it with all your heart, as working for the Lord, not for men, since you know that you will receive an inheritance from the Lord as a reward. It is the Lord Christ you are serving.

Living to please God results in a life that is pleasing to others and finds great pleasure in inner peace and confidence.

OTHER PLEASURES

All of this is not to say that we as believers will never know any immediate pleasure or ecstatic sense of joy. God provides many pleasurable experiences within the framework of His will. We feel pleasure when we ponder His works (Psalm 111:2): a dramatic sunset, the majestic mountains, the smile of a baby, an answer to prayer, or a manifestation of His grace or power.

We feel pleasure as our hearts, heads, and lips respond to all that God has done for us. As a result, we express our worship and praise, sometimes in bold, unabashed singing and rejoicing, and at other times in quiet, reflective joy with tears of gratitude welling in our eyes. The children of Israel danced for joy when God delivered them from Egypt at the Red Sea, as did David when the ark of the covenant was restored to Jerusalem.

We so often equate the sacred with the solemn. But you can't muzzle the joy of the Lord with chants and ritualistic responses. When His pleasure is felt, we might just "shout for joy to the Lord" and "worship the Lord with gladness" (Psalm 100:1).

God has also made us to experience many other legitimate pleasures as we live to please Him. There is the pleasure of work and its productive accomplishment, the pleasure of food, the pleasure of sex within the intimacy of marriage, the joy of friends, laughter, and play. Redemption does not deny pleasure, but delivers it with a depth and power that can be enjoyed without delusions or despair.

Concerning work and pleasure, Solomon declared:

A man can do nothing better than to eat and drink and find satisfaction in his work. This too, I see, is from the hand of God, for without him, who can eat or find enjoyment? To the man who pleases him, God gives wisdom, knowledge and happiness, but to the sinner he gives the task of gathering and storing up wealth to hand it over to the one who pleases God. (Ecclesiastes 2:24–26)

We must remember that God seeks to grant us pleasure. Christ reminded us that it is the Father's good pleasure to give us the kingdom (Luke 12:32) and that He gives us all things to enjoy (1 Timothy 6:17). A redeemed and redirected pleasure instinct is an energy that keeps us moving toward God's glory and gain, and denies our adversary a foothold to lure us back into a life obsessed with the pleasure of our own significance.

The pilgrim song of redirected pleasure is:

> *Living for Jesus a life that is true,*
> *Striving to please Him in all that I do;*
> *Yielding allegiance, glad-hearted and free,*
> *This is the pathway of blessing for me.*[4]

If there were a biblical Declaration of Independence, it would declare that every person has the right to find pleasure in God and to bring pleasure to God by obeying Him and serving others.

Strange but true: We maximize our pleasure when we focus it on Him—His glory and His gain—and when we minimize impulses to bypass Him in an effort to find pleasure apart from God.

CHAPTER NINE

THE FALL OF PRIDE

The story of Joseph Stalin's prideful, deathbed defiance of God may be the most extreme example of human pride out of control, or rather under the control of Satan. But unredeemed pride is just as dangerous and destructive for us in other areas of life.

God takes our pride seriously. How we handle or fail to handle our pride instinct helps to determine the direction our lives will take. History holds plenty of examples for us to learn from. Let's try to understand what this energy is, and how it can be refocused to promote God's glory and gain.

With anger, vengeance, and a proud heart, Joseph Stalin murdered thousands of his enemies. Even those who gave only lukewarm allegiance were branded "enemies" and killed. Many others were sent to Soviet prison camps for slave labor, torture, and an early death in the gulags. I have spent time with pastors who endured brutal treatment in Siberian prison camps. If Scripture were to comment on Stalin's deepest motivation, it would talk about the issue of pride.

Simply put, pride is the assumption that I am the most important person in my world—more important than other people and institutions, and even more important than God. Pride is the "in your face" attitude of the soul. This assumption that self is preeminent manifests itself in arrogance, insolence, and boasting. When threatened, pride can become violent and treacherous. Self is the focus of pride. Pride seeks to defend and advance self in every way possible.

Pride is inextricably linked to our significance obsession. In fact, pride is the engine that drives the obsession. This inflated notion of self-significance contributes to almost every negative response in life. When someone crosses or belittles us, pride triggers retaliatory and defensive mechanisms that seek not only to protect but to exact revenge.

Pride is the real reason we rarely admit we are wrong or seek forgiveness, and it may be the reason we refuse to extend forgiveness to those who have hurt us. Pride not only tends to cripple relationships by pitting people against each other, but it is also at the root of much of our violence and social unrest. When pride is accurately understood as the preeminence of self, we can see why rape is possible, sexual abuse a reality, and abortion an option for many.

My pride ignites the quest to make my rights supreme. This quest gives rise to many strident and divisive movements in our society in which groups seek not just their place, but dominance over other groups. It is what drives racism and the violent reactions to racism. At the base of Adolf Hitler's destruction of millions was the twisted pride of supposed Aryan superiority. In Hitler's mind, the belief that he and his race were preeminent gave them the right, even the responsibility, to exterminate "inferior" races.

No one wants to be identified with things like this, but both social chaos and the cold-blooded maneuvering of the marketplace find their roots in the same struggle we all feel to advance ourselves—our own significance—at all costs. When this happens people are not valued, but used as stepping-stones that someone walks on in his climb to the top. No option is ruled out as a tool of this surging energy in our souls.

THE POWERFUL PULL OF PRIDE

We have seen that pride was a key player in the whole scenario surrounding the fall of man, and even prior to that as Lucifer sought to be like God. Discontent with his exalted position, he later tried to make Adam and Eve discontent with theirs. He succeeded, luring the pair with a promise that they could be more significant—they could be like God.

No one is exempt from the powerful pull of pride. Some show their pride in obvious, showy demonstrations, such as Soviet premier Nikita Khrushchev, who in 1960 declared to America, "We will bury you," and pounded his shoe on a desk at the United Nations, or like boxer Muhammad Ali who proclaimed his greatness to my generation. "I float like a butterfly, sting like a bee" he intoned in self-congratulatory rhyme; he predicted in which round his opponent would fall and reminded all who would listen, "I am the greatest." Most of us, however, are too civilized to be so outgoing about our pride. We maneuver for acclaim or self-advancement in more subtle yet just as calculating ways. As children, we may make eye contact with one of the softball team captains, hoping he or she will call our name to join the team; as adults we may fish for compliments. In subtle ways we jockey for space, recognition, and affirmation.

Until we get to the other side, we will all struggle to keep the alligator of pride down in the swamp of our lives. This reptile of the soul tends to express its passions selectively, in places where it is sure it will be safe and successful. In this regard pride is a cowardly attribute. We rarely seek to advance ourselves when we think we are with people who are more powerful than we or capable of putting us in our place. Some of us have controlled pride enough to appear quite humble and modest among friends (particularly if they are religious friends), and yet we can be absolute wretches at home, demanding that everyone play our tune and exploding in anger when people try to change the song.

Recently someone asked me, "How do you handle pride?" He assumed that the position I hold must be fraught with great temptations to pride and self-enlargement. As I thought about it, I realized that the position God has called me to does not seem to swell large within my spirit. In fact, except for my mother, probably no one is more surprised than I that I serve as the president of Moody Bible Institute. I am still awe-struck as I walk through the legacy-laden arches of our campus and wonder, *Why would God call me to do this?* Perhaps it is God's insulating grace around my life and the realization that if I did not hold this sovereignly assigned position, very few people, perhaps nobody, would ever pay much attention to me.

But as I continued to think about the question, I realized that I do struggle with pride in different arenas. For instance, I fight pride in certain kinds of relationships where I want to be sure my rightful place is maintained and affirmed. I fight pride every time I want to be liked and appreciated and when I find it difficult to be crossed. Pride makes me defensive. Pride urges me to perform well for the wrong reasons and to be noticed, and even admired, in conversations.

I find pride licking its chops over me sometimes in traffic. I'm amazed at what happens in my spirit when someone cuts me off or refuses to let me in. As far as I'm concerned, the other driver has devalued me and imposed his power over me. My thoughts in moments like that are less than honorable.

Sometimes pride takes us dangerously close to disaster. If it gets carried away, pride can move us beyond safe boundaries in expressing its outrage. Sitting at a red light recently, I watched two cars go through the intersection. A blue Corolla seemed to be chasing a red Grand Am, blaring its horn constantly and driving nearly bumper-to-bumper behind the red car. At first I thought the driver of the Corolla was trying to flag down her friend in the car ahead. I turned right, and at the next red light I ended up next to the two cars. The woman in the Toyota climbed out, stormed over to the Grand Am, and started banging on the window.

"Don't you ever cut me off like that again!" she screamed. Then this woman, about 5 feet 8 inches, shouted something bad about the driver's mother, with a few other insults thrown in for good measure, and stormed back to her car. At this point, a tall, powerful-looking man got out of the red Grand Am and walked back to the woman's car as she climbed behind her steering wheel. I thought to myself, *She is going to get in her car, roll up the windows, lock the doors, and pretend like it never happened.* But to my shock, she got back out of her car and stood on her tiptoes right in his face, screaming more insults with seemingly no fear or realization of the danger she was in.

It was pride at its best and its worst. The man shouted something back at her, and then decided to walk away, which was a humble response given his size advantage. He got into his car and pulled the door closed. But the woman marched in front of his car, crossed her arms, and stood there while the rest of us left, since the light had turned green!

Pride gurgles like a boiling cauldron in the depths of our souls, often boiling over, scalding others as we seek to advance, defend, or maintain our significance. Pride's raised fist, however, is not primarily against people or institutions. It is, first and foremost, an affront to God.

WHEN PRIDE PREVAILS

As we have learned, our pleasure instinct assumes that it can completely satisfy its cravings apart from God. In a similar way, the pride instinct rises up and competes against the rightful place that God should hold in our lives. By definition, God is supreme, the ruler of everything, giver and supplier of all. Thus, He has the singular right to be worshiped with the totality of every person's life.

SELF ABOVE PRIDE

But pride makes the arrogant claim that I am more important— more important than the God of the universe. It is an individual's "in your face" statement to God. Every time I do what I want to do and ignore what He requires me to do, I am elevating my importance over His Lordship. Every time I ignore God's Word, His will, and His way, I am saying that something else is more important to me than God.

Society at large, particularly in North America, has tried to erase God from its collective memory. The theory of evolution seeks to eliminate His fingerprints from creation. If He is not really the Creator, then He may not be there at all, and we are free to do what we want.

Society has also tried to scrub God out of all public discourse, reducing Him to the status of an outsider whose advice is at best only one voice among many. The heresy of our day is that religion is purely a private matter. If someone wants to believe in God that's his private business. But let him keep his religion to himself. We'll manage society and culture the way we see fit. This is a clear reflection of our cultural pride.

Pride's effort to displace God from His rightful position should strike fear into the hearts of those of us who are biblically sane. Who among us would ask God to step aside so we can fill His place or sit on His throne? Yet, that's what the arrogance of pride in effect causes us to do. It is the instinct not to let God be God, so that *self* can be God!

How ugly is pride? The psalmist answers that for us:

> In his arrogance the wicked man hunts down the weak, who are caught in the schemes he devises. He boasts of the cravings of his heart; he blesses the greedy and reviles the Lord. In his pride the wicked does not seek him; in all his thoughts there is no room for God. His ways are always prosperous; he is haughty and your laws

are far from him; he sneers at all his enemies. He says to himself, "Nothing will shake me; I'll always be happy and never have trouble." His mouth is full of curses and lies and threats; trouble and evil are under his tongue. He lies in wait near the villages; from ambush he murders the innocent, watching in secret for his victims. He lies in wait like a lion in cover; he lies in wait to catch the helpless; he catches the helpless and drags them off in his net. His victims are crushed, they collapse; they fall under his strength. He says to himself, "God has forgotten; he covers his face and never sees." (Psalm 10:2–11)

Pride breeds quarrels, and it is found in the mouths of fools ((Proverbs 13:10; 14:3). God also says that pride leads to self-deception (Obadiah 1:3–4). We delude ourselves by believing that we are invincible. We deceive ourselves by believing that we do not need God, and that we can make it on our own. The apostle Paul warned that those who are lifted with pride fall into the condemnation of the devil (1 Timothy 3:6).

Thus, it is easy to understand why God speaks so strongly against the pride that raises self in an effort to displace Him. In fact, pride appears in every major list of evil things in Scripture. For instance, in demonstrating that the heart of mankind is inherently wicked, Christ declared,

What comes out of a man is what makes him 'unclean.' For from within, out of men's hearts, come evil thoughts, sexual immorality, theft, murder, adultery, greed, malice, deceit, lewdness, envy, slander, *arrogance* and folly. All these evils come from inside and make a man 'unclean.' (Mark 7:20–23, my emphasis)

In Romans 1 Paul included in his characteristics of the world those who are "filled with every kind of wickedness, evil, greed and depravity," those who are "God-haters, insolent, *arrogant* and *boastful*" (vv. 29–30, my emphasis). Paul warned Timothy regarding the end times:

People will be lovers of themselves, lovers of money, *boastful, proud,* abusive, disobedient to their parents, ungrateful, unholy, without love, unforgiving, slanderous, without self-control, brutal, not lovers of the good, treacherous, rash, conceited, lovers of pleasure rather than lovers of God. (2 Timothy 3:2–4, my emphasis)

Perhaps most sobering and even frightening, however, is the list in Proverbs 6:16–19 that begins, "There are six things the Lord hates, seven that are detestable to Him." Leading the list are "haughty eyes," which means a person who looks at life through proud eyes. The other six things God hates are direct results of a proud spirit. In this context it is frightening to think that our lives might be characterized by pride.

SHAME AND LOSS

Scripture also clearly reveals that those who permit their lives to be ruled by self-focused pride end up with shame and loss. Here is probably the greatest irony of our fallenness: the very thing we use to catapult ourselves upward is the thing that brings us low. When pride rules, shame is the result (Proverbs 11:2). There's a reason that Proverbs 16:18 is one of the most famous verses in the Bible. Proverbs 29:23 issues the same warning: "A man's pride brings him low."

Even a casual reading of history verifies the tragic impact of this truth. Hitler sought to elevate himself and His Nazi empire over all the world, and to oppress all those below him. His proud life, though, ended in shame, misery, and self-inflicted death.

Sometimes the shame is recorded after one's life is over. Joseph Stalin lived and died with his fist raised in the face of God, but Nikita Khrushchev led a purge of Stalin's influence and even memory that was so complete it was called destalinization. Stalin was erased from Soviet history, his statues were toppled, and Stalingrad was changed to Volgograd in 1961. The empire he gave his life to build is now gone, and his name is a byword for inhumanity.

Interestingly, Khrushchev himself suffered a fate similar to Stalin's. A few years after pounding his shoe on the table of the U.N. General Assembly, Khrushchev was removed from power and banished to obscurity.

We should remember that the most revolting sin of Sodom was not the people's sexual perversion but their pride, according to Ezekiel 16:49. They refused God's rightful supremacy in their lives, and so they felt free to do all they wished.

Advanced in culture and located in a fertile valley, Sodom was a proud city. Its people rejected the righteous influence of one of its residents, Lot, and when it came time to judge the city, not one person had submitted his life to the supremacy of God. In a moment God's judgment fell on the city, which is today a byword for detestable acts of sexual perversion.

In the course of our lives, shame and failure always follow in the wake of our attempts at self-advancement. It may be the guilt and regret that sin always brings when pride supplants God and permits sin to have its way. Or it may show itself simply as shame and embarrassment as we stumble while trying to promote ourselves and feel the ridicule of those around us.

SELF-GLORY

Perhaps the most debilitating aspect of pride is that it makes us competitors to the glory of God. Only God is worthy of glory and honor. Self-glorification competes with that. It seems almost ludicrous to imagine that the creature would even think he could have greater glory than the Creator. Yet we often do just that. No wonder the psalmist declared, "Ascribe to the Lord, O mighty ones, ascribe to the Lord glory and strength. Ascribe to the Lord the glory due his name; worship the Lord in the splendor of His holiness" (Psalm 29:1–2). Throughout the psalms, David and other writers reiterated the supreme person and power of God. We should affirm with them, "Not to us, O Lord, not to us but to your name be the glory" (Psalm 115:1).

God does not take lightly those who seek to rob Him of the glory that is rightfully His. Once Nebuchadnezzar, the king of Babylon, had seen God's power in delivering Shadrach, Meshach, and Abednego from the fiery furnace, he declared "to the peoples . . . who live in all the world: . . . How great are his signs, how mighty his wonders! His kingdom is an eternal kingdom; his dominion endures from generation to generation" (Daniel 4:1, 3).

Later, however, Nebuchadnezzar was again deluded by visions of greatness and proclaimed in a fit of self-adulation, "Is not this the great Babylon I have built as the royal residence, by my mighty power and for the glory of my majesty?" (4:30). This direct, prideful competition with the glory of the Almighty God was met with swift retribution:

The words were still on his lips when a voice came from heaven, "This is what is decreed for you, King Nebuchadnezzar: Your royal authority has been taken from you. You will be driven away from people and will live with the wild animals; you will eat grass like cattle. Seven times will pass by for you until you acknowledge that the Most High is sovereign over the kingdoms of men and gives them to anyone he wishes." Immediately what had been said about Nebuchadnezzar was fulfilled. He was driven away from people and ate grass like cattle. His body was drenched with the dew of heaven until his hair grew like the feathers of an eagle and his nails like the claws of a bird.

At the end of that time, I Nebuchadnezzar, raised my eyes toward heaven, and my sanity was restored. Then I praised the Most High; I honored and glorified him who lives forever. His dominion is an eternal dominion; his kingdom endures from generation to generation. (Daniel 4:31–34)

Once the king affirmed God's rightful place in history, God restored his kingdom and his earthly glory. Clearly, God takes seriously those who try to compete with His glory. Nebuchadnezzar's confession reminds us of another truth about God's glory: He will entrust earthly honor, power, and possession only to those who recognize that He is the giver of their glory and the One who can also take it away.

Herod Agrippa, king of Judea, never learned that lesson. When he accepted the crowd's acclamation, "This is the voice of a god, not of a man" and "did not give praise to God, an angel of the Lord struck him down" (Acts 13:21–23). Those who think that they can stay the power and plan of God by the flex of human will are doomed to disappointment and defeat. We come back to the declaration by the apostle Peter: "God opposes the proud but gives grace to the humble" (1 Peter 5:5).

PRIDE REVISED

It is pure fantasy, the ultimate fantasy, to think that there is no God, or that if He is there, He is irrelevant and we are free to do as we please. It's also a fantasy to believe that by the elevation of self, mankind can construct anything that won't self-destruct. People were never built to run on their own. We were built to recognize God for who He is, to worship and glorify His name, and to live joyfully under His Lordship.

Without some kind of redemptive revision to our pride instinct, pride can take back the ground we have gained in our liberation from our significance obsession and throw us again into the old self-seeking and self-serving patterns. It may be safe to say that of all our internal energies, pride most resembles our addiction to our significance. Pleasure functions to satisfy self, and passions feed on our longings for significance. But it is pride that is dedicated to the magnification of our significance.

It's understandable why a committed pagan would never think twice about the problem of pride. There is no God in his life. But for those of us who have been redeemed, allowing ourselves to be managed and manipulated by pre-redemptive pride makes no sense. Pride will throw up great roadblocks at the most strategic times, detouring us as we try to fulfill our redemptive purposes. When that happens, we cannot glorify God and live for the gain of His kingdom as He intends for us.

Like other professional sports, football has become big business in America. With huge player contracts and the gate receipts that winning teams collect, filling stadiums and making it to the playoffs have become important parts of NFL competition. But the object of the game remains the same: once your team has the ball, you advance it toward the goal line. The team that crosses the goal line most often during sixty minutes wins. It's that simple.

Of course, there is more to it than that. Football is a tough, get-beat-up experience that takes more than resolve and sophisticated strategies. There's another team with huge linemen who are committed to stopping you cold and getting the ball back. When it comes to redemptive advance, pride is like that. Redemption has put us on the right team. God has delivered us from the small backyards of our own significance and has put us on the only playing field that counts—the gain of His glory and kingdom. And it's the only game in town.

But across the line from us are massive defensive players, motivated by Satan himself. Thankfully, the pleasure platoon has just been signed by our team. It has come to our side of the line, throwing its power toward finding pleasure into bringing pleasure to God. Our pleasure instinct now helps us move forward for God's glory. Yet, planted in front of us is this huge defensive line of pride. But its charge can be repulsed and pride can be revised, as we will see.

Our pride instinct cannot be defeated. Rather, it must be refocused toward its intended goal: empowering our lives toward God's glory and gain. If pride is not refocused—recruited to play on our side of the line—it remains fully capable of picking us up and throwing us back every time. No one wins when pride is working against us.

CHAPTER TEN
PRIDE REVISED

Can pride be redeemed and made to work for God's glory? Despite all the evidence around us, God's Word says that it can. The good news is that the solution to unredeemed pride is not suppression or eradication. Like our pleasure and passion instincts, pride is part of our created makeup.

Bringing the "pride platoon" over to our side of the field is a matter of getting God's perspective on pride and understanding His intended purpose for its proper expression.

The pride platoon loves to wreak havoc on us. What can we do, then, with this force that resides so powerfully in our hearts? Our first impulse is to try and eradicate it. We reason that we can kill pride through some act of our will. After a strong sermon on pride, we awake Monday morning resolving to renounce pride, to delete it from our agendas. "I will live today without pride," we declare. Others wake up and say, "I will adopt in its place the quality of humility," which we rightly assume is the other side of pride. But we soon find that the struggle remains.

The reality is that no one can escape pride. As usual, C. S. Lewis described pride as well as anybody:

> There is one vice of which no man in the world is free; which every one in the world loathes when he sees it in someone else; and of which hardly any people, except Christians, ever imagine that

they are guilty of themselves. . . . The essential vice, the utmost evil, is Pride. Unchastity, anger, greed, drunkenness, and all that, are mere fleabites in comparison: it was through Pride that the devil became the devil: Pride leads to every other vice: it is the complete anti-God state of mind.[1]

Since pride is so revolting, some seek to express humility by being quiet, not smiling much, and certainly not laughing loudly. We impose on our spirit a mellowness; with great tenderness we try to be sure that we put everyone else far out in front of us, and never once do we value who we are. This is humility, we tell ourselves. We try to talk slowly and carefully, never raising our voices in excitement and certainly never expressing any point of view that may be important to us, particularly if the issue is controversial. And most important, we lace our sentences with spiritual talk at every opportunity.

Many of us assume the posture of doormats, and as we respond weakly and solemnly, we welcome foot traffic to walk across our lives. I suspect that most people would say, "If this is what it takes to defeat pride and convert it to the right side of my life, if this is humility, I think I'll pass on this spiritual project, have one less reward, and go on to a different spiritual challenge."

But I have good news. That kind of humility is not what God demands. In fact, His Word never tells us to eradicate pride and assume a wimpish demeanor. Pride is an expression of something that has been created deep in our souls to give us the power and capacity to honor and advance God's kingdom.

PROPER PRIDE

Pride is that part of ourselves that we call ego. Men take a particularly bad rap in this area, but I don't know a woman who would want to have a man with no ego either as a friend or a life partner. Most women are not enthralled with passive manhood. The issue for all of us, men and women, is whether our egos are Spirit-directed. If our egos with their determination, energy, and power are directed by God's Spirit—so that we are energetic, enthusiastic, and insistent about God's glory and gain—we've got a powerful force for good. At that point, the pride platoon has come over on our side of the line and is playing ball with us for God's glory.

REVISED, NOT REPLACED

So the issue is not pride eradicated, but pride revised. Our pride must be refocused to honor Him. True humility is a life that has put pride in its place.

Pride has many self-focused manifestations that are always out of bounds: arrogance, insolence, violence, boasting, and other forms of self-elevation. Scripture, however, describes certain aspects of pride in positive ways. When this energy within is refocused on the magnificence of God, instead of the magnificent *me*, we are compelled to praise and serve our marvelous Maker.

The prophet Jeremiah said:

> This is what the Lord says: "Let not the wise man boast of his wisdom or the strong man boast of his strength or the rich man boast of his riches, but let him who boasts boast about this: that he understands and knows me, that I am the Lord, who exercises kindness, justice and righteousness on earth, for in these I delight," declares the Lord. (9:23–24)

Jeremiah understood this redemptive refocus. Notice that the one who called for boasting here was God Himself. But it is pride that's properly placed, not in ourselves but in Him who deserves our attention and affirmation.

THE FATHER'S GLORY

In the intriguing French film entitled "My Father's Glory," a husband and wife living in Paris take a vacation in the countryside with their two boys and the boys' aunt and uncle. Upon arrival, it becomes apparent that Marcel, the older boy, deeply admires his dad. He is embarrassed that his uncle dominates and intimidates his father. Early one morning, the two men go hunting. Marcel begs to go with them and although his father seems to be weakening, his uncle firmly says that this is not something for a boy to be doing. As the men leave, Marcel sneaks off and follows them from a distance.

As the hunters walk through the valley chatting and looking for quail, he walks along the ridge, hiding behind bushes when he thinks they might see him. Quite by accident, Marcel flushes two royal partridges out of the bush. As they rise, his father spots them and raises his gun, as does his uncle. But Marcel's father is faster, and fires twice. Both birds come plummeting to the ground at Marcel's feet.

Ecstatic at his father's triumph, Marcel grabs the quail and lifts them high, one in each hand, and his shouts echo through the hills: "He killed them, both of them. He did it!" As the camera zooms away from the boy, the gorgeous beauty of the hills and valley envelops him as he stands, arms lifted with quail in hand, raising his father's glory to the sky.

It is that kind of revised pride that marks authentic believers. No longer consumed with ourselves, we realize that we belong to the Creator, and as we behold the marvel of His works and wisdom we find our hearts swelling with pride that He is our Father and we are His children. We lift our voices instinctively in worship and praise to His unsurpassed glory. Pride revised is pride turned Godward. It is not arrogant, insolent, or self-absorbed. It is the energy within stirred by the greatness of our God. It is the energy that catapults us to glorify God.

TRUE HUMILITY

The book of Philippians was written in response to the "Judaizers," people who emphasized the law in the community of Christ and encouraged those redeemed by grace to fulfill their redemption by keeping the law. This heresy had a devastating impact on the Philippian church in many ways. One was that it created a caste system among the believers, between those who conformed to the rites and rituals of the law of Moses and those who did not. Those who did tended to boast of their advanced status and look down on those who did not. Here was pride busy at work in the early church.

Speaking of the Judaizers, Paul warned, "Watch out for those dogs, those men who do evil, those mutilators of the flesh" (3:2). Then he focused on authentic Christianity: "For it is we who are the circumcision, we who worship by the Spirit of God, who glory in Christ Jesus, and who put no confidence in the flesh" (v. 3). His exhortation was to resist the sense of pride that comes when we place our confidence in human accomplishments (by keeping the law). Instead, we should fix our pride in Jesus Christ as we "glory in Him."

Interestingly, Paul then listed his credentials, the things of which he could have been proud: "circumcised on the eighth day, of the people of Israel, of the tribe of Benjamin, a Hebrew of Hebrews; in regard to the law, a Pharisee; as for zeal, persecuting the church; as for legalistic righteousness, faultless" (vv. 5–6). But he refused to allow these things to become a platform for pride. Instead,

> Whatever was to my profit I now consider loss for the sake of Christ. What is more, I consider everything a loss compared to the surpassing greatness of knowing Christ Jesus my Lord, for whose sake I have lost all things. I consider them rubbish, that I may gain Christ and be found in him, not having a righteousness of my own that comes from the law, but that which is through faith in Christ— the righteousness that comes from God and is by faith. I want to know Christ and the power of his resurrection and the fellowship of sharing in his sufferings, becoming like him in his death. (vv. 7–11)

Paul counted his relationship with Christ to be of far greater importance than anything else, so he determined to spend his life rejoicing in Him. No longer proud of himself, Paul was infinitely proud of the finished work of Christ, the One who loved Paul and gave Himself for Paul. The wonderful possibility is that if all of us in the body of Christ refocused our pride on Christ and sought to elevate Him, we would all find release from the divisiveness of striving for position and celebrating our own accomplishments.

What, then, is true humility? It's not an act of our wills—something we manufacture—but a by-product of being consumed with Christ's supremacy. When we are enthralled with all Christ is, we begin naturally to display the elements of humility: praise, obedience, trust, and prayer.

PRAISE

A proper view of the greatness of God cannot escape the reality that we are the created and that all we have is by Him, from Him, and for Him. There is no such thing as a self-made person. The psalmist caught this truth when he proclaimed, "Know that the Lord Himself is God. It is He who has made us and not we ourselves; we are His people and the sheep of His pasture" (Psalm 100:3 NASB).

We are not only created by Him with all the capacities to perform and succeed; the text claims that we also belong to Him. Property resounds to the glory of the owner. Although a house or a car can be admired in and of itself, when the owner comes by, the glory and attention naturally focus on him or her. Similarly, when others observe our attitudes and actions, we need to give credit to our owner and maker. Our identity and our glory are found in Him. We are His sheep, totally dependent for provision and protection; we thrive only in His pasture. Our praise for all of this will give honor and glory to His name.

It is safe to say that there is not an aspect of our lives that is not due to Him. Seeing this marvelous reality about God, David, the great king of Israel, declares, "Enter His gates with thanksgiving, and His courts with praise. Give thanks to Him; bless His name. For the Lord is good; His lovingkindness is everlasting, and His faithfulness to all generations" (Psalm 100:4–5 NASB).

Seeing God as Creator and Provider prompts the humble response of tactfully and creatively giving Him the glory for all we are and do. Whether in worship as we sincerely praise Him or in our actions with others who commend us, giving God the credit due His name is humility at its best.

Whether like Marcel who refused to take credit for kicking up the quail but rather consumed himself with his father's glory, shouting his father's praise for all to hear, or like my Hebrew professor who told the bank teller that it wasn't that he was an honest man but that Christ had changed his life, praise is the natural response to pride focused away from self and to God where it rightly belongs.

No wonder Scripture says, "Through Jesus, therefore, let us continually offer to God a sacrifice of praise—the fruit of lips that confess his name . . . for with such sacrifices God is pleased" (Hebrews 13:15–16).

OBEDIENCE

The second element of genuine, biblical humility is obedience. Pride enthrones itself in the temple of the will. But once we understand Christ's rightful place as the Ruler of the universe and Lord of our souls, we yield ourselves to Him. Since He is God, every contest of the will is really no contest. When we fully understand all that He is, obedience should be a natural response.

Two passages of Scripture demonstrate this dynamic of humility. In Exodus 10, Moses and Aaron approached Pharaoh and said, "This is what the Lord, the God of the Hebrews, says, 'How long will you refuse to humble yourself before me? Let my people go, so that they may worship me'" (v. 3). Pharaoh was the ruler of the great Egyptian empire and had the right to call the shots in his domain, but God was the supreme Ruler who had a right to demand Pharaoh's obedience. It wasn't as though God hadn't demonstrated His power to Pharaoh. Plague after plague made it clear that the Egyptian monarch was up against a far greater God. Yet Pharaoh refused to humble himself before God.

How unlike Christ, of whom Paul said, "He humbled himself and became obedient to death" (Philippians 2:8). Humility is measured in our unconditional obedience toward Him.

TRUST

The third dynamic of humility is the ability to trust God to work for His glory. Such humility means trusting God to deal with situations that are beyond our control. It was said of Moses, who held a high and prestigious position as Israel's leader, in Numbers 12:3 that he was "a very humble man." In the face of tremendous opposition, he refused to retaliate or defend himself, but was willing to rely on God to intercede on his behalf.

Our Savior also exhibited the capacity to patiently trust God to work on His behalf. While on earth, time and again, when confronted by lies, distortions, and temptations, He maintained a righteous balance trusting His Father to ultimately vindicate His life and ministry. Early in His ministry He rejected Satan's efforts for Him to claim His Messianic glory by going outside God's plan to demonstrate His power. When Satan called on Jesus to throw Himself down from the highest point on the temple, Jesus had the opportunity to accelerate God's timetable for the kingdom (Matthew 4:5–7). When the temple guard and the elders came to arrest Him, Jesus submitted readily, even though He had the power to call more than a dozen legions of angels to aid Him (Matthew 26:50–53). Even as impatient Peter drew a sword to defend Jesus, the Messiah accepted God's plans for betrayal and death because He trusted His Father's ability to see Him through. As the writer of Hebrews says of Christ, "who for the joy that was set before Him, [He] endured the cross."

Before Pilate, Jesus refused to argue with His accusers, remaining silent and amazing Pilate (Mark 15:3–4). The charges were trumped-up lies by false witnesses, but Jesus knew He did not need to defend His name or enhance His reputation by delivering Himself. Instead in humility He trusted God His father to do what was best—and walked the road to Calvary. That road lead to death—but also to resurrection power.

Trusting God to work all things together for good gives us the humility to forgive our enemies. Trusting Him to do justice toward them who have treated us unjustly releases us from proud acts of revenge and enables us to humbly love and serve even our enemies (Matthew 5:43–48; Romans 12:17–21).

PRAYER

Waiting for God to show Himself powerful is not always easy. But if we trust Him enough to obey Him, we will readily go to Him in prayer.

In fact, prayer is the fourth element of humility. In 2 Chronicles 7:14 we read that those who "humble themselves and pray" win God's approval. Prayer is reliance on another. Whether it be the worship of an adoring heart or the intercession of a broken life, prayer recognizes God as supreme and gladly comes to Him to find mercy and grace to help in the time of need.

Clearly, God views our humility with rightful pleasure. He doesn't wish our competition. In fact Scripture teaches that although He resists the proud He gives grace to the humble and guides them and crowns them with His rescuing power.

HUMILITY AND COMPETITION

Sometimes we give the impression that if we are truly humble, we will not be competitive in terms of setting goals and seeking to reach them. But whether it be in the marketplace, in our personal lives, or in our families, we need to remember that humility does not mean passivity. In fact, a passive humility is really a pagan notion. Those who seek to be humble without God are simply self-deceived and rightly deserving of the world's scorn. But when our humility is a response to the supremacy of God, we live to glorify Him and to succeed that He might be glorified in us and His kingdom advanced through us.

Many business people who have accomplished great things are also enthralled with the supremacy of God. They give Him credit for what they have and do. Being successful, they capture the attention of others in the marketplace, and as those who would emulate them get close they see something more than the Christian businessperson's material success. They see in these Christians' lives the supremacy of God. And God receives honor and there is gain for the kingdom.

HUMILITY AND VULNERABILITY

Some may also think that a genuinely humble life will be vulnerable and unprotected. But if we have yielded to God and are willing to live for Him, we can trust His power and wisdom to deliver us in His time. Because God gives grace to the humble, the apostle Peter's advice is sound: "Humble yourselves, therefore, under God's mighty hand, that he may lift you up in due time" (1 Peter 5:6).

Once we refocus the pride platoon, it becomes a helpful team member in the advancement of God's glory and the gain of His kingdom. When we submit ourselves to God's supremacy, pride becomes our helper, for we glory in Him and gladly obey.

The sequence is best described in Romans 11:33–12:3, where Paul described in awestruck tones the wonder of God (11:33–36), then issued this call:

Therefore I urge you, brothers, in view of God's mercy, to offer your bodies as living sacrifices, holy and pleasing to God—which is your spiritual worship. Do not conform any longer to the pattern of this world, but be transformed by the renewing of your mind. Then you will be able to test and approve what God's will is—his good, pleasing and perfect will. For by the grace given me I say to every one of you: Do not think of yourself more highly than you ought, but rather think of yourself with sober judgment, in accordance with the measure of faith God has given you. (12:1–3)

Here is true humility, a proper attitude about ourselves that comes from understanding the greatness of God, our value before Him, and our inadequacy apart from Him. No wonder we want to obey and give Him glory. He is worthy of it all.

We learned as Sunday school children that if you take the "big I" out of pride, there's nothing left. That old adage has a lot of truth to it, assuming as it does that we're talking about pride apart from God, focused on self and seeking to advance self at all costs.

But pride has a place in our lives—pride revised and refocused on Christ, that is. With Him as the focus of our pride, we can harness pride's tremendous energy to do things that bring glory to Christ and advance His kingdom. Humility, in fact, is merely pride properly placed!

CHAPTER ELEVEN

PASSION IN PERSPECTIVE

> *Life wouldn't be much without passion. On a hot, steamy day it's the passion for a double-dip strawberry ice cream cone that drives us to enjoy one. Longings are the passions of our souls that link us to the basic things we need. Hunger is a longing that keeps us alive. We have longings to procreate that attract us to the opposite sex. Longings for friendship and fellowship drive us to cultivate meaningful, productive relationships.*
>
> *We were created with primary, vitally important longings in our souls. Most important of all, we are built to long for God.*

CBS News anchorman Dan Rather was on our Moody campus some time ago for Moody Broadcasting Network's national program, "Open Line." Rather would answer questions regarding the supposed anti-Christian bias in the media. During his visit, I had a chance to chat with Rather about traumatic world events of the moment—the Persian Gulf War, the fall of the Berlin Wall, and the phenomenal openness in the former Soviet Union that glasnost and perestroika had made possible.

Mr. Rather said that years ago in talking with Billy Graham, he had told the evangelist "The communists have succeeded in obliterating religion." Dr. Graham replied that they had only oppressed religion, not obliterated it.

"I'm surprised at the tremendous surge of interest in God and religion in the independent states of the former Soviet Union," Rather admitted. "Obviously Billy Graham was right."

"It does seem surprising, doesn't it?" I said, as we continued to chat. "But every person is built for a relationship with God, giving us an intrinsic longing for Him."

Though the Soviet people had been denied the freedom to worship for more than a half century, their desire for God never had been extinguished. And that should not be surprising. We were made to long for God. This longing was created in us that we might be drawn to God and satisfy our lives in Him. We are built to enjoy a relationship with Him. That is part and parcel of what it means to be created in His image. We have the capacity for fellowship with God through our will, emotions, and mind.

When that fellowship is severed, as it was in Eden, these capacities reach out like tentacles, searching for satisfaction wherever it can be found. If these longings do not find satisfaction in God, they will attach themselves to lesser, sometimes destructive, things. While these things may bring momentary satisfaction, we are left with a lingering emptiness because our deepest longings can only be met by redemptive reunion with God.

Longings are the drive and motivation within us to link us to life's essential realities. When Martie and I first met in our freshman year of college, she intrigued me. I was drawn to her and desired to know and understand all I could about her. That early, primal longing of my soul has developed over the years into a deep longing that continues to motivate me to link my life fully and wonderfully with hers.

When I travel, though the trip may be exciting and full of the fast pace of business and ministry that I love and thrive on, it's not long before the joy of the trip wears off and my heart longs for Martie and home. This longing takes me home at the end of a trip with a sense of joy and anticipation.

BASIC LONGINGS

The fall of Adam and Eve severed man from God and pushed the panic button on our passions, sending us on a desperate search for fulfillment. But the Fall did not change the fact that we were created with a few basic longings that travel with us through our earthly lives. As noted in chapter 2, we were built with the passions to procreate, rule, and provide. These passions, however, are part of a larger scheme of passions that interplay into our energies: a longing for God, for others, and for the land.

A LONGING FOR GOD

The most fundamental of these larger longings is our longing for God. This innate longing draws us toward Him and enables us to seek and maintain a fulfilling relationship with Him. It opens the door of our lives to His power and joy and to His reflection through us. As Oswald Chambers observed, "The one great passion of the saint is that the life of the Lord Jesus might be manifested in his mortal flesh."[1]

As God's image-bearers, we were built for this kind of satisfying relationship with Him. And even though God is transcendent, He seeks a relationship with us that we might be His children and that He might be our God and Father.

This longing for God impacts how we manage our longings to procreate, rule, and provide. When we permit our passion for God to control our daily relationship with Him, we will direct those three subpassions in ways that glorify God. And our whole perspective on the second larger passion—others—will be rearranged as well.

A LONGING FOR OTHERS

The second fundamental longing we are created with is the longing for other people. Genesis 2 describes that marvelous moment when God, having pronounced that it was not good for Adam to be alone, caused a deep sleep to fall on him. Isn't it interesting that there was a part of Adam's makeup that even a passionate relationship with God did not fulfill? Adam needed someone like himself. So God took part of Adam and formed someone like Him—not a duplicate, but someone who would wonderfully complement him.

I have often tried to imagine the scene. Adam wakes up from his sleep, rubs his eyes, and as he gets up and looks around the familiar garden, standing near him is this someone he has never seen before. There must have been an exclamation of surprise and pleasure as he was astounded at how beautiful and how much like him, yet how much unlike him, this provision of God was.

According to Genesis 2:22, God made the introductions, and Adam responded with delight, "She shall be called 'woman'" (v. 23). The text then comments, "For this reason a man will leave his father and mother and be united to his wife, and they will become one flesh" (v. 24). It is clear that they were built for each other, and that there would be a natural desire to leave all else and cleave to each other.

As the human race multiplied and the world filled with other people, relationships and friendships developed, meeting our longings for human fellowship. The New Testament underscores the importance of this longing through the metaphor of the body of Christ. If you want a fascinating and rewarding Bible study, trace the "one another" passages that fill the pages of the New Testament. They encourage us to fulfill this relational longing in ways that are fruitful and glorifying to God. We are to love one another, be kind to one another, encourage one another, edify one another, and care for one another, to name just a few.

A LONGING FOR THE LAND

The third passion that God has created in us is a longing to relate to the land—to the environment around us. In Genesis 1:27–30, God left no doubt that the material creation is designed for our benefit. Throughout history, mankind has had a passion to subdue, care for, and enjoy God's marvelous creation. In every culture, this passion has led people to cultivate, gather, enjoy, and find significance in the creation.

Our God-given longing to care for and enjoy His created order is expressed in many ways. We cultivate the land, not only to produce food, but to beautify it with grass, flowers, trees, and other things of beauty that bring us satisfaction and joy when we step back and look at what we have produced.

We were created, then, to long for God and other people in a place where we can find satisfaction as His stewards. But if we are not careful, these passions can quickly become disorganized and distended. To help prevent that, God assigned a hierarchical system for their management, a system that would assure our fulfillment. It's reflected first in Genesis 1:28–30, where mankind was assigned dominion over the earth. Then in Genesis 2:15–17 it is recorded that:

> The Lord God took the man and put him in the Garden of Eden to work it and take care of it. And the Lord God commanded the man, "You are free to eat from any tree in the garden; but you must not eat from the tree of the knowledge of good and evil, for when you eat of it you will surely die."

It is clear from this passage that God is to be the primary focus of our passions. Under His direction we can focus on relationships with others, and then together we can manage and enjoy His creation within the boundaries and guidelines He has established for procreating, ruling, and providing.

ENTER THE ADVERSARY

It is exactly at this point that our adversary entered the scene and sought to tamper with the divinely-arranged management of our passions. We keep coming back to Genesis 3 because it is so foundational to everything we're talking about. Satan knew that to capture both man and the created order for his destructive purposes, he would have to appeal to these divinely-placed longings and use them to seduce the governors of the earth. The adversary knew that if he could seduce Adam and Eve in this way, he could distort their lives and destroy their relationship with the Almighty.

And so the adversary got our first parents to long for something outside the boundary of God's will, and we all know the rest of the story, both theologically and personally. Man and woman linked their passions to something other than God. Eve was seduced to long for the created order more than for her God. For Adam it was a little different. He had enjoyed unhindered fellowship with God for a longer period of time than Eve, and he was the one to whom the command not to eat of the fruit was given. Adam's point of seduction was not the created order, but his created other: Eve, this one who had become so intimately significant to him.

This primal pair stand as vivid reminders of our struggle to refocus our passions and restore them to their pre-Fall perspective. For some of us, it is the material world that seduces and distracts us, and that distorts our longings for God. For others, it's the people around us whom Satan uses to distract us from our longing for God. It may be our friends or our enemies, a man or a woman. When these seductions lure us away from loyalty to God, our longings to procreate, rule, and provide get out of their intended focus.

As soon as Adam and Eve crossed God's boundary, everything changed. Because of their sin they were now hopelessly separated from Him, and the joy of His fellowship was replaced by fear of His presence. They felt legitimate shame and guilt, and when God came back to the garden after they had mismanaged their passions, their longings drove them not to Him, but into hiding. Yet God in His marvelous grace reached out to them in a process of restoration that was intended in part to reestablish their longings according to His original plan.

Since mankind's fall into sin, there has been an additional longing in the human heart: for restoration. Ever since God banished Adam and Eve from the garden, mankind has longed for Eden again. Longed for home. Longed for heaven. C. S. Lewis says in *Mere Christianity,*

> Most of us find it very difficult to want "Heaven" at all—except in so far as "Heaven" means meeting again our friends who have died. One reason for this difficulty is that we have not been trained: our whole education tends to fix our minds on this world. Another reason is that when the real want for heaven is present in us, we do not recognize it. Most people, if they had really learned to look into their own hearts, would know that they do want, and want acutely, something that cannot be had in this world. There are all sorts of things in this world that offer to give it to you, but they never quite keep their promise. The longings which arise in us when we first fall in love, or first think of some foreign country, or first take up some subject that excites us, are longings which no marriage, no travel, no learning can really satisfy. I am not now speaking of what would be ordinarily called unsuccessful marriages, or holidays, or learned careers. I am speaking of the best possible ones. There was something we grasped at, in that first moment of longing, which just fades away in the reality. I think everyone knows what I mean. The wife may be a good wife, and the hotels and scenery may have been excellent, and the chemistry may be a very interesting job: but something has evaded us.[2]

That which Lewis speaks of, that thing which has evaded us, that gnawing in our soul, is the longing for restoration to the fullness Adam and Eve enjoyed in Eden, where their longings for God, for each other, and for the land were perfectly satisfied. In Eden, procreating, ruling, and providing coexisted peacefully, and man and woman were fulfilled. Today, even though we are redeemed, we will not be complete until we have crossed to the other side. Composer Don Wyrtzen's song "Finally Home" says it so well:

> Just think of stepping on shore and finding it heaven!
> Of touching a hand and finding it God's!
> Of breathing new air and finding it celestial!
> Of waking up in glory and finding it home![3]

But that is just our problem. While we long for home, for the fullness of God's presence, we're not there yet. We still live amid the seductions of the world, and Satan time and again seduces us into longing for its lesser and sometimes lurid thrills. He may use the material world or people to seduce us, but his strategy is always the same: to distract and distort our passions, and then lead us to the destruction that results from longings which look for fulfillment in all the wrong places.

LONGINGS AND LUSTS

In Scripture, legitimate longings that are mismanaged, that are allowed to go beyond the boundaries God has set, are called *lusts*. We have seen that there is nothing wrong with passion. It's a matter of perspective, focus, and management. Scripture says that our lusts grow out of our fallenness. Sin rearranged us, rendered us dead before God, severed us from the satisfaction of His fullness, and sent us on a wild chase to find a lodging for our longings. And we should remind ourselves that it's not the lusts around us but the fallen passions within us that we struggle with.

This is what the apostle James spoke of when he said that the process of sin and destruction begins within (1:13–15). He concluded with this important warning: "Don't be deceived, my dear brothers" (v. 16). Our society offers us a phenomenal array of outlets to plug our passions into, whether it be food, sex, friendships, money, success, or a dozen other enticements. But the destructive pattern does not begin until we accept Satan's offer and seek to fulfill our passions in the wrong way. Being enticed by our lusts we are led into sin, and sin then brings destruction. It's the adversary's familiar pattern in regard to our longings: first distraction, then destruction.

We can appreciate James's warning when we recall that Satan first had to deceive Eve about the character of God before he could distract her and destroy both her and Adam. The adversary convinced her that God was stingy and restrictive, that He was holding out on her. If Eve would just wake up to this fact, her longings could be satisfied in a much more full and meaningful way.

Satan tries to distract us in similar ways. He wants us to believe, for instance, that our pursuit of God to fulfill our longings will be unsatisfying and difficult, that the quick fixes and emotional kicks readily available to us are much more satisfying and enhancing to our pride and pleasure. When we are distracted from God as the primary focus of our longings, when we stop seeking Him and begin seeking lesser things as sources of satisfaction, then the distraction turns to our destruction.

LONGINGS AND THE FLESH

We need to remember that we can't have it both ways. The apostle John said that those who long for the world through the lust of the flesh, the lust of the eyes, and the pride of life are incapable of loving God (1 John 2:15). Longing for God and longing for the mismanaged passions of our souls are mutually exclusive. But when we long first and foremost for Him, He helps us manage our passions and their relationship to others around us and to the material order. It keeps us within God's boundaries and opens us to the wonderful world of pro-creation, rule, and provision without regret.

But if we reverse the flow and long for that which is lesser and even lurid, though we may give lip service to God, our longing for Him is gone. Every time that happens, we push ourselves to the brink of disaster. As we have learned, every seduction to fulfill our own wants and needs apart from God brings us shame, regret, guilt, loss, and emptiness. It's an inescapable truth: "The one who sows to please his sinful nature, from that nature will reap destruction" (Galatians 6:8).

The link between lust and flesh is important to note. John called our passions "the lust of the flesh" (v. 16, KJV*). *Flesh* is used in the New Testament as a metaphor for our sinful nature. Two things are important to note about the flesh. The first is its outcome: "The acts of the sinful nature are obvious: sexual immorality, impurity and debauchery; idolatry and witchcraft; hatred, discord, jealousy, fits of rage, selfish ambition, dissensions, factions and envy; drunkenness, orgies, and the like" (Galatians 5:19-21). This catalog of corruption speaks clearly to the destructive influence of a life whose longings are outside the boundaries of God's intended purpose.

The second thing to note about the flesh is that it's in direct competition with the work of God and His Spirit in our lives. Galatians 5:17 tells us that our flesh and the Holy Spirit are set in opposition to each other. The closing portion of the verse sums up the struggle for every believer: "They are in conflict with each other, so that you do not do what you want." As we seek to bring our passions back into line with their intended purpose, we will often meet tremendous internal opposition since it goes against the grain of our old systems of behavior.

But this change of focus is the goal for those who have been redeemed and liberated from their addiction to their significance. Only when we succeed in the redemptive restructuring of our passions will we know true fulfillment in our longing for God. Like pleasure and pride, our passions, when restored to their intended purpose, become allies in our goal to glorify God and serve His kingdom.

REVERSING THE FLOW

How do we reverse the flow so that our passions undergo a redemptive restructuring? The processing of our passion instinct is much like what the city forefathers did in Chicago decades ago. The Chicago River runs directly through the city and in the early days was a source of transportation and commerce. Originally it was like every other tributary of Lake Michigan, flowing from its source into the lake with all of its accumulated debris. The lesser (the river) contributed to the greater (Lake Michigan), most often contributing pollutants and particles that defiled the lake.

---

*King James version.

So engineers got the idea that if they could reverse the flow of the Chicago River so that the power and resources of Lake Michigan would flow into it, then it would always have a guaranteed source of supply. The water from the depths of the great lake would be fresh and clean, and flowing from the greater to the lesser would be a source of long-term satisfaction and strength to the city.

The engineers did just that. They reversed the flow of the Chicago River so that today it is the only river in all of the Great Lakes system that receives its water from the lake. Because of this the river is clean, strong, and never lacking for a source, unlike tributaries that draw their water from lesser and often unreliable sources like rainfall, snow melt, and underground springs.

Unfortunately, some of us are like the Chicago River before its flow was reversed. We have never permitted God's Spirit to restructure our passions, to draw our satisfaction from God and His clean resources. As a result, our passions draw their fulfillment from the world around us, and all we have to contribute is the debris and pollution we have accumulated. If you have ever flown across the Louisiana bayous where the Mississippi River meets the Gulf of Mexico, you know that the beautiful, pristine, deep-blue waters of the Gulf are dirtied for miles as the Mississippi dumps its debris into the greater body of water. Sadly, a bird's-eye view of Christianity at times looks like that, with the pollutants of misplaced passions spilling into the sacred seas of church, home, and friendship.

To reverse the flow and to restructure our longings, we must realize first that though a tremendous capacity to long for Him remains, there are things we have cultivated that distract us and cause us to long for lesser things. Once we realize that we have the redemptive potential to rekindle our longings for the God who can satisfy our deepest longings, we must prune away those distractions. When we do, we can say with the psalmist, "As the deer pants for streams of water, so my soul pants for you, O God. My soul thirsts for God, for the living God. When can I go and meet with God?" (Psalm 42:1–2). Having our deep thirst for God fully satisfied in Him should be the goal of our lives.

FOUR FATAL DISTRACTIONS

The Scriptures mark for us those things that interfere with our longing for God and smother its too-often flickering flame. Scripture indicates at least four fatal distractions that can quench the longing for God in our hearts.

The first distraction is *willful sin in our lives*. We have already seen how the sin of Adam and Eve quenched their longing for God and replaced it with fear. The more you and I permit sin to escalate, whether it be a momentary rebellion or determined disobedience over a long period, the more it will smother the longing for God that was rekindled at redemption.

Dealing with sin demands consistent repentance and an unabashed commitment to righteousness regardless of the cost. This deepening intimacy will fan the flame of our longing for God. We don't long for those we fear. We long for those with whom we have cultivated deep and lasting friendships.

Second, Scripture indicates that our longing for God can be detoured by *the distraction of abundance*. God issued Israel an interesting warning in Deuteronomy 8. He told His people He was bringing them into a good land where they would be abundantly cared for and "lack nothing" (v. 9). But then came the warning (vv. 10–14). In essence, God warned the people not to forget who gave them all they had. In the presence of plenty, the Israelites faced the same temptation we face: to let these lesser things fill our hearts so that we cease to long for what is truly significant, our relationship with God.

The tragedy of plenty is not the wealth itself, but the fact that we forget the One who has given us what we have (v. 18). The answer is not to decide to live in poverty, because that doesn't deal with the longing for wealth. The issue is not how much we have, but disciplining our hearts to remember that God is the one who has graciously provided what we have, will be there if we lose what we have, and remains of far greater value than anything we will ever have (Hebrews 13:5–6).

Those of us who have been seduced by affluence need to rethink our values and refocus our hearts in praise and thanksgiving to God for the abundance He has given to us. We need to practice the discipline of reveling in and celebrating the Giver more than the gift, and use His supply as a means to glorify His name and advance His kingdom.

The third distraction that seeks to seduce our longings is *our struggle with self*. We examined this issue earlier through the eyes of Paul, who had a very impressive list of human credentials (Philippians 3:4b–6).

What's amazing is how thoroughly he renounced them (vv. 8–9) in favor of his relationship with Christ, one to which Paul brought nothing but his sin and received everything by grace. For Paul, Christ was far more valuable than any earthly accomplishment. No wonder the focus of the great apostle's life was, "That I may know [Christ] and the power of his resurrection and the fellowship of sharing in his sufferings" (v. 10).

Sometimes we read this passage and conclude that Paul was talking about a level of spirituality reserved for apostles, prophets, and patriarchs. But what Paul was talking about is intended to be the normal Christian life. We cannot revel in a longing for Christ when we are consumed with longing for our own advancement. People who long for *me* have a hard time longing for *Thee*.

The fourth distraction that tends to quench our longing for God is a subtle one: *allowing our walk with Christ to become ritualized and systematized*. Those of us who have been around the kingdom for years know all too well how easily this can happen. When our faith becomes a system more than a Savior, a ritual more than a relationship, then our longings become legalized and the passion is frozen by meaningless practices.

Why do we serve as choir members, ushers, Sunday school teachers, and committee members at church? Do we serve because it's the thing to do, or because someone asked us? Do we avoid sin because we're afraid of the consequences, or so we won't disappoint our parents, spouses, children, or pastors? Do we give because we know that if we do, God may give back to us in greater measure and our prosperity will be abundant? Do we serve as pastor because that's what we've been trained to do? Do we serve as elders or deacons because we enjoy the high profile and the power?

These and a dozen other reasons are the wrong ones to be involved in the work of Christ. And yet we so quickly come to the place in our Christian life where service is not a passion, but a project. Have we forgotten when we used to do what we did because we loved Christ and wanted to express that love?

When He is the center of our work and worship, He remains the longing of our lives. But when living for Him becomes a list of chores, Christ becomes our burden and not our passion. It must have been like this in the church at Ephesus, to whom John wrote on behalf of the risen Christ:

> I know your deeds, your hard work and your perseverance. I know that you cannot tolerate wicked men, that you have tested those who claim to be apostles but are not, and have found them false. You have persevered and have endured hardships for my name, and have not grown weary. Yet I hold this against you: You have forsaken your first love. Remember the height from which you have fallen! Repent and do the things you did at first. If you do not repent, I will come to you and remove your lampstand from its place. (Revelation 2:2–5)

The thought of "first love" here is not time, but priority. The first-priority love of my life is to Jesus Christ, and out of that love I'm stimulated to do all that I do. Then He is no longer a function, but a friend. No longer a burden, but the blessing of our lives.

Cultivating a passion for Christ means unlayering our lives in regard to sin, surplus, self, and religious systems. As we apply scriptural disciplines in these four areas, our redirected passions should be reconnected so that we find ourselves longing for Him and Him alone.

Liberated by the redemptive work of Christ on the cross, we find our significance in Him. We discover true pleasure in pleasing Him and others. We learn the intended fulfillment of pride when we are so awe-struck with Christ that we're proud beyond description of Him. Then we focus our passions on Him, finding our satisfaction in nothing else. This is liberated living!

Listen to Oswald Chambers once more: "Passion is usually taken to mean something from which human nature suffers; in reality it stands for endurance and high enthusiasm, a radiant intensity of life, life at the highest pitch all the time without any reaction."[4] *That's what awaits us when we focus our God-given passions on Him and find them fully satisfied.*

REFLECTIONS
ON REFOCUS

1. What brings you the most immediate pleasure in life? What kinds of things or activities bring the most long term, lasting, regretless, fulfilling pleasure to your life?

   Do you see any correlation between your answers and the kind of righteousness that is pleasing to God?

2. Are you a people pleaser? If so, who do you feel compelled to please?

   Are you tired of trying to please others, of living life like a popularity contest?

   Have you ever thought of refocusing your pleasure instinct toward pleasing God and creating a life that is free from the debilitating downside of pleasure for pleasure's sake?

   How would you feel if you knew your life brought pleasure to God and as a result brought pleasure to others?

   What are a few beginning ways that you could plan to bring pleasure to God with your life?

3. Can you isolate the specific arenas in which self-focused pride is most prevalent in your life?

   How do these manifestations of self-focused pride compete with the redemptive purposes of God's glory and gain?

   How could you change those competitive moments to moments in which God's glory is revealed in your life?

4. Reflect on what you know to be true about God. When you look at God as He really is, are there areas in which you think you are better or even close to Him? Obviously not. God in His marvelously expansive person is far beyond even the best parts of us. If you were to focus your sense of pride on His greatness, what would be different about your life?

   Realizing the supreme greatness of His works, ways, and Word, and His goodness to us, have you responded with a desire to glorify Him by giving Him the credit for all that you are and have?

   Does your awareness of the greatness of God prompt you to obey and trust?

   In what specific areas do you struggle with obedience? With trust?

   Think about those areas. Is God not greater, more worthy than that temptation?

   Is His hand weak that He cannot help, or is He fickle that He does not care? Or can you trust as you sing "Great Is Thy Faithfulness"?

5. What are the accomplishments of life that you are most proud of?
   What did God provide in your life that enabled you to accomplish those realities?
   Who deserves the credit?

6. What do you long for in life?
   Is God on the list? On top of the list?
   Check the four distractions that compete with our longing for God: abundance (or the desire for it), self-promotion, ritualized religion, and sin. Which of these bury your longing for God?
   What can you do in each of these areas to lift the layers that smooth your longing for God?
   Set your heart on longing only for Him.

PART FOUR
RESPONSE

CHAPTER TWELVE

TAKING THE INITIATIVE: SURRENDER AND SACRIFICE

Finding our secured significance in a restored relationship to God, and transitioning the instincts of pleasure, pride, and passion to constructive energies, set the stage for us to take the initiative in fulfilling His intended purpose for our lives. This is the focus of our fourth and final section: response.

In His earthly life and ministry, Christ clearly lived for the glory of His Father. Christ sets the pace for us, as He models a fourfold response in a life free from a significance obsession that is the example for us. In this chapter we'll explore the first two of these commitments: surrender and sacrifice.

The little village was so small and remote that we were the first foreign visitors to come there in thirty-eight years. We sat in a simple little home some sixty miles from Minsk, Belarus, with one of the students who had come to MBI from the former Soviet Union, his mother, and his pastor. I listened to Pastor Ivan tell of his work in that area and watched the movements of his battle-lined face. I was unprepared for the story he told, but I will never forget its impact on my life. Here was an unsung hero who has been faithful through many years of oppression and difficulty.

During the severe oppression of Russian believers under Stalin, this pastor, then a young man, was asked by the Soviet secret police, the KGB, to report on the affairs of the congregation to the secret police while still serving as pastor. The state would take good care of him, and no one would know. As I listened to Ivan, I wondered what I might have done had I been in his shoes. This was an opportunity for safety and security for this pastor and his family, and also an opportunity to share in the significance of being a part of one of the world's most powerful forces.

Obviously, though, Ivan was a man who had long before found his significance in Christ. He was free to look those KGB agents in the eye and say no. "No, I cannot do that to my Lord or my people." He knew that his refusal to betray Christ for a ticket to his own significance would probably earn him arrest and a ticket to a Siberian labor camp. And that's exactly what happened. Put on a ship with fifteen hundred other prisoners, he was off to Siberia on a journey during which six hundred prisoners died in a boiler explosion on the ship. He was force-marched across the frozen, windswept Siberian tundra to the prison camp where he arrived with most of his shoe leather worn away from the forced march. He served there for ten years.

"Were there any other Christians in your camp?" I asked, and the interpreter translated.

"Yes. We would get together often to read the Word to one another, encourage one another, and sing hymns of praise to God. During the last few years of our imprisonment, we were sent out in a sixty-mile radius from their camp to help build towns in the Siberian wilderness for Stalin.

"As we went to these remote places, the Christians would gather in fellowship. Often we were able to share our faith quietly with the people in the villages." He paused, with an obvious sense of satisfaction and joy on his face, then added, "You know, today there are literally hundreds of churches all over Siberia as a result of those fellowship groups of Christians during those ruthless years of the oppression."

I listened to this remarkable story, marveling at the power of God that can take a person committed to the glory of Christ and the gain of His kingdom, and use him so dramatically for the advance of the gospel. It was as though God, in His desire to establish outposts in the

Siberian wilderness, said to Stalin, the dictator who railed against God, "Take some of My finest servants, those who are not addicted to their significance but to My work, and send them as missionaries to Siberia. And you pay the bill!" And so some of God's finest were sent off, not knowing why they went, but simply being faithful to God.

A FOURFOLD COMMITMENT

Being free from our obsession to our own significance and having refocused the energies of pleasure, pride, and passion toward God releases us to follow a fourfold pattern of commitment that makes us wonderfully usable in the Lord's hands. Through this pattern God has used parents, janitors, presidents, and kings to bring glory to His name and accomplish great things for Himself. In fact, it is the very pattern that Christ followed when He accomplished our redemption, the greatest gain for God's glory and plan that has ever been accomplished. This is the commitment of those who want to take the initiative and position themselves to be used by God.

Here are the four essential commitments that Christ lived out in His earthly ministry and His death on the cross to purchase our redemption. He was willing to surrender to the Father's will, willing to sacrifice His privileges and position, willing to serve, and willing to suffer.

Without those four essential commitments, Christ could not have taken the initiative to accomplish the great work of redemption and secure its benefits for us: hell canceled, heaven guaranteed, and the redeemed being made fully significant in the Father, free to advance and enhance God's glory through Christ's power in us.

The commitments are most fully described in Philippians 2. Verses 3–4 help to set the context for us, a fascinating one in which we are exhorted to abandon our addiction to our significance: "Do nothing out of selfish ambition or vain conceit, but in humility consider others better than yourselves. Each of you should look not only to your own interests, but also to the interests of others."

It is important to note how absolute the exhortation is. We are to do nothing out of self-advancing motives. Nor are we to focus only on those things that benefit us. I think it would be interesting if, for one day, we kept track of the number of times we were either tempted to—or succumbed to the temptation to—do, say, or think something that deliberately served our significance only.

We would probably be shocked at how full the page would be. There would be entries noting the times we jumped into a conversation to look or sound important and intelligent, or just to elbow our way into the discussion. Other entries would record the times we said no to someone else's need because it conflicted with our need; the times we bent truth to protect or enlarge our significance in other people's eyes. There might be an entry or two noting our resentment at someone who achieved a higher level of significance than we did, or how we let our thoughts spill out in gossip or slander. I could go on, but you get the idea.

In sharp contrast, Paul calls on us to adopt the mind of Christ. Instead of being consumed with ourselves (Philippians 2:3–4), we should, "Let this mind be in you which was also in Christ Jesus" (v. 5, KJV). Then in verses 6–8 we come to the fourfold mindset that Christ committed Himself to in order to accomplish His Father's glory and plan for His life:

> Who, being in very nature God, did not consider equality with God something to be grasped, but made himself nothing, taking the very nature of a servant, being made in human likeness. And being found in appearance as a man, he humbled himself and became obedient to death—even death on a cross!

THE PATTERN OF CHRIST

What better way to display our liberation from an obsession with our own significance than to pattern our lives after Jesus Christ, who is far and away the most significant One in the universe (Colossians 1:14–18). If Christ, who had every right to celebrate and advance His significance, could take the initiative to accomplish His Father's glory by submitting Himself to this vital fourfold process, then the implications for us are profound. How can we, who have no intrinsic significance in comparison to Christ, refuse to serve our Father's glory and His gain by seeking to advance and enhance ourselves? We can't! That's why the authentic, liberated follower of God adopts the pattern of Christ. Let's look at the first two components of this fourfold commitment.

STEP ONE: SURRENDER

Step one in taking the initiative to fulfill our redemptive calling is a willingness to surrender to an agenda bigger than ourselves—to God's agenda. Philippians 2:6–8 makes it clear that Christ was willing to get beyond the power, privileges, and perks of His supreme position in the universe and commit Himself to His Father's gain and glory.

Surrendering to God's agenda in and through us requires a clear view of the agendas we have prescribed for ourselves. Most people's lists of things they consider important would include personal peace, happiness, comfort, prosperity, security, friends, good health, fulfilling experiences, and reaching their full potential.

The above list should make the need for our surrender obvious, for those plans often conflict or ignore God's plan for us. It's true that God may and often does provide for us measures of peace, prosperity, position, fulfillment, and other things on our lists, but our surrender to God's plan is a statement that we will not live for these things. They are not the things that drive us, but are simply side benefits that come through the sovereign pleasure of God.

Let's never forget the great benefit to God's glory and kingdom that has come through the lives of thousands of people who have surrendered to agendas beyond their own. Some have gone to faraway lands as missionaries. Mothers have surrendered careers and opportunities for significance to teach their children God's truth. Fathers have changed careers or turned down promotions that conflicted with God's will for them or their families. Pastors have faithfully served in out-of-the-way places where no one knows their names or asks them to speak at high-profile conferences.

Surrendering to something greater than ourselves reminds me of the time that D. L. Moody first heard the rich, full voice of Ira Sankey at a Sunday school convention. In his trademark direct way, Mr. Moody went to Sankey and said, "I have been looking for someone like you for years. You must leave your position at once and join me in my work in Chicago."

Sankey protested that he already had a job in Cincinnati, but it was to no avail; Moody persisted, and Sankey finally realized he had to surrender to a plan greater than his own. He joined Moody in Chicago, and the pair became the greatest evangelistic team of the nineteenth century.

Earlier in this century, a young Bible college graduate responded similarly to the call of God. He intended to start a church in the Upper Peninsula of Michigan where, in those days, the logging camps were brutal places to live and work. Going into one of the camps, he tried to start by inviting the children of the town to Sunday school. He went door-to-door in the toughest part of town, where even the police refused to patrol, looking for children for his Sunday school. Most of those doors were slammed in his face, but two boys, Les and Jay, asked their mothers if they could go. Week after week, year after year, that pastor drove into the tough part of town and picked up those boys for Sunday school.

Les and Jay eventually accepted Christ, were discipled under his care, and when it came time to go to college they too, like their pastor, went to Bible school to train for ministry. Upon graduation, Jay Walsh sensed God's call to become a missionary in Bangladesh, a land where very few missionaries had gone. Jay forged a ministry in Bangladesh that established a base for the effective spread of the gospel.

Meanwhile, back in the States, an agnostic doctor was led to the Lord and dedicated the rest of his life to medical service for Christ. He wanted to use his skills to serve in a place where there was little medical help and a great need for the gospel. So Dr. Viggo Olson found himself on his way to Bangladesh, following in the steps of Jay Walsh. While there, Dr. Olson wrote the story of his conversion and surrender to missionary service that became the best-selling book, *Daktar*. Many doctors were influenced for Christ through the book, and hundreds of young people, after reading it and hearing Dr. Olson's testimony, gave their lives to the cause of world missions.

Les Ollillia, the other boy from that Michigan logging town, became a youth evangelist. Les moved to the Midwest, presenting the gospel to young people until God tapped him on the shoulder to become the president of Northland Bible College in Wisconsin, where he is multiplying his surrendered spirit in the lives of many young people who will replicate his commitment around the world.

It's amazing what God can do through one pastor, unknown and unheralded in an obscure logging camp—and uninterested in his own significance—who surrenders himself to the glory of God and the gain of His kingdom. Your surrender may not take you into career ministry. Your calling may be in the marketplace as someone who views a career not as an opportunity to accumulate wealth, position, and power, but as an avenue whereby you can glorify Christ and advance His kingdom by your influence.

My friend Clayton Brown, founder and chief executive officer of Clayton Brown and Associates, one of the leading bond houses in Chicago, recently told me over lunch that although he could sell his business, retire, and be comfortable for the rest of his life, he wasn't ready to do that yet. Why? Because he knew that the day he sold his business, he would lose his ministry in the Chicago Loop.

Clay has held weekly Bible studies in the Loop for years, and today there are business people who know and live for Christ because of those studies. Young people regularly seek Clay's advice as to how one meshes business and a commitment to Christ, and he helps them. Clayton Brown is a man who has surrendered to an agenda beyond himself.

This kind of commitment has marked God's people for generations. Susanna Wesley, whose pastor husband was busy in the ministry and not very involved at home, gave birth to nineteen children, of whom only nine lived to adulthood. She reared her children for the most part single-handedly. It was said that Susanna gathered with her children every day for two hours to read Scripture, pray with them, and teach them the things of God. Her years of faithfulness paid off when God used two of those children—John and Charles Wesley—to bring revival to the British Isles and fill our hymnals with hymns that continue to bless us to this day.

Stack up the results of lives that have been committed to God's program rather than to personal comfort and convenience, and the comparison is dramatic. If the mind of Christ is to be ours, we must gladly surrender ourselves in every area of life to His glory and gain through us. God calls us to surrender to His agenda in the arenas of our money, our motives, our time, and our attitudes. He calls us to surrender to His agenda at home and in the marketplace. There is no segment of life where surrendering self to serve His glory and gain does not apply.

STEP TWO: SACRIFICE

Philippians 2:6–8 reveals a second commitment of Christ's that must be ours as well. It was a willingness to sacrifice in order that God's will might be accomplished through His life. What a stunning truth: even though Jesus was God, He did not cling to the privileges of His position. Instead, He willingly emptied Himself (v. 7). Although we will never understand fully all that this tremendous sacrifice meant for Christ, we can see several levels at which He emptied Himself to come and redeem us.

The first level of sacrifice was that of His privileges and rights as the God of the universe. Emptying Himself meant that Christ had to give up the voluntary use of many of His attributes. For instance, He yielded His omnipresence to be confined in the body of a baby, and His omnipotence to endure the cross without overpowering His enemies with ten thousand angels. Christ also sacrificed the "perks of paradise"—the glory, praise, and honor bestowed upon Him by the angelic hosts, all the splendor of what it meant to be Creator, Sustainer, and Ruler of the universe—to be born in a lowly stable while the world slept unaware.

Jesus even sacrificed things that ordinary humans expect to enjoy in the course of life: the reliability of intimate friendships, being understood and accepted for who He was, having a place to lay His head, and a little money in His pocket. Ultimately, Christ made the most intense sacrifice of all: giving His body to be hung on the cross like a criminal, having the sins of the entire race heaped upon Him, and dying the death of a despised outcast.

The bottom line is this: Christ voluntarily emptied Himself of anything and everything that stood in the way of the glory and gain of His Father through Him.

What about us? Although rights, privileges, pleasures, possessions, expectations, and well-formed plans may not be wrong in and of themselves, are we willing to hold them loosely and even let them go—to sacrifice them—if emptying ourselves of them will enable us to fulfill God's agenda for our lives?

I find it interesting that as we challenge this generation with the unsurpassed cause of spreading the gospel, we have no trouble exciting teens and young adults to seriously consider giving themselves to career ministry, and enlisting them for training in schools like Moody. Our problem is with parents who get their kids off to the side and caution them about going into something that is not a "solid, stable" career, who urge their children to get a "real job" and then maybe God will use them to help others do what they're contemplating doing at this point.

Surrendering to God's agenda may mean sacrificing our children—or our goods, reputation, comfort, convenience, and a whole list of other things we hold so tightly in our hands as well as those things we hope and plan for.

I think back to Jesus Christ's call to Peter, Andrew, James, and John to follow Him. To obey, they had to let go of their fishing nets. I've often wondered about the "nets" of money, people, plans, things, and comfort in our hands that inhibit us from making a full commitment to following Christ. Those things may be valuable to us. But in the light of who Jesus Christ is, they become insignificant next to His glory and eternal gain. The issue for us is whether, like the disciples, we are willing to let go of our nets for the sake of Christ's work.

Sacrificing *our* sense of significance to magnify Christ's significance may pose many strategic challenges. Several years ago, while our family was preparing for a vacation trip to Florida to visit grandparents, I got bad news from our mechanic. The transmission in our old car was in no shape for a drive all the way to Florida. It would have to be repaired first. That would have been fine, except that we were leaving the next day. The mechanic told me the soonest he could get the work done was the middle of the next week, effectively canceling our vacation.

As I sat at my desk mulling over the disappointing news, the phone rang. It was a man in our church who had heard that we were going to Florida and was concerned about our whole family traveling in our undersized car. He had no idea of the transmission problem.

"Pastor, God has been good to my wife and me, and one of our joys is to be able to share God's blessings with others. We'd like you to take one of our cars for your trip to Florida. You pick the car."

Both cars were very nice and certainly a major step up from what we had planned to drive. So I chose a car, and we happily packed our family in and left for Florida.

This was one of those cars that turns heads on the highway. I have to admit that I've rarely felt so significant—in the fallen sense of the word—as when I drove that Lincoln Town Car to Florida.

On the way home, we stopped for gas at the self-serve pumps. *Self-serve* seemed a contradiction in terms for a car like that—I doubt that it had ever been to a self-serve pump before. As I stood there pumping the gas, I noticed a man standing by the pumps staring at the car. He walked over, looked admiringly at the car, and asked me, "How do you like your car?"

That was a tough question to field, because I didn't want to tell him that it wasn't my car. It seemed like the war raged in my soul for a long time, although it was just a few seconds. Would I be willing to sacrifice my undeserved sense of significance to magnify the integrity of Christ through my life? I knew what I had to do. "Well, it's not my car, but I like it very much."

Frankly, that wasn't much of a sacrifice compared to what we are called to sacrifice on many other occasions to magnify Christ's name and advance His cause. But for me it was a rather dramatic reminder of how tough it is at times to sacrifice our significance, which seems so compelling, and surrender to an agenda beyond ourselves.

> *We can step out for Christ and become participants in the glorious agenda He has for us—to glorify Him through our lives and accomplish great gain for His kingdom. Though we will sometimes struggle against relapses into our significance obsession, the liberating power of Christ enables us to embrace the commitments of surrender and sacrifice that make us greatly usable to Him.*

CHAPTER THIRTEEN

TAKING THE INITIATIVE: SERVANTHOOD AND SUFFERING

> *After Christ had emptied Himself of anything that could hinder His expression of God's glory, He took upon Himself the "very nature" of a servant and "became obedient to death—even death on a cross!" (Philippians 2:7–8). A willingness to serve and to suffer if necessary are the final commitments we must make as we take the initiative to glorify Christ and accomplish what He has called us to do.*

I n Matthew 20, after the other ten disciples became incensed that James, John, and their mother had asked for places of honor in the kingdom, Christ called the twelve disciples together. He informed them that although the world operated by trying to gain personal power, position, and status, in His kingdom it would not be so. "Instead, whoever wants to become great among you must be your servant, and whoever wants to be first must be your slave—just as the Son of Man did not come to be served, but to serve, and to give his life as a ransom for many" (vv. 26–28).

We must remember that Christ came with a commitment to servanthood. If He had come to serve His desires and needs, the glory and gain of redemption would never have taken place. Servanthood is a vital element of the committed Christian who finds his significance in God alone.

STEP THREE: SERVANTHOOD

Christ drove home the issue of servanthood dramatically as He met with the disciples in the Upper Room on the night before His crucifixion. They had come for a last meal of intimate fellowship with their Lord. The only thing missing was the hospitality custom of foot-washing, when a servant would meet guests at the door with a basin of water and refresh them by washing their feet, which typically had walked the hot Palestinian roads. We can imagine each of the disciples glancing around, waiting for someone else to do such a lowly job.

TOWEL, PLEASE

Then, in a dramatic moment that became a metaphor of His redeeming servanthood, Christ got up, laid aside His robe, signifying the yielding of His privileges, put a towel around His waist, which was the sign of a servant, drew a basin of water, and washed each of the disciples' feet. Then He went back to His place and said, "Do you understand what I have done to you? . . . You call me 'Teacher' and 'Lord,' and rightly so, for that is what I am. Now that I, your Lord and Teacher, have washed your feet, you should also wash one another's feet. I have set you an example that you should do as I have done for you" (John 13:12–15).

To anchor this truth in their minds, He went on to say that slaves are not greater than their masters. His point was inescapable. If He came to be a servant, then those who worship Him and call Him Master must be prepared not to elevate themselves, but to pick up the towel and basin of servanthood for His glory. Servanthood is our willingness to do whatever it takes to accomplish the best for another person. It means serving the purposes of God through our lives, and it is the essential identity of an authentic Christian.

Most of us know that God has called us to servanthood; however, allowing ourselves to be identified as servants goes against the grain of our expectations for significance. It also violates the misdirected energy of pride. No one really wants to be known as a servant. A friend of mine who serves as a missions executive once was flying coast to coast at the hospitality of another person. This person had provided him with a first-class ticket, my friend's first trip in the up-front seats. As he reclined in the comfort of his leather seat, he noticed that across the aisle from him was an older couple who were obviously very wealthy—"old money," as they say.

As the flight began, a flight attendant made her way down the aisle and said to this older woman, "Ma'am, would you like a pillow?" She looked straight ahead without answering. Thinking that perhaps the plane's engines were a little too loud, the flight attendant raised her voice and repeated her question. Still no response.

So, assuming that the woman was hearing-impaired, the attendant said in a voice that could be heard throughout the first-class cabin, "Ma'am, would you like a pillow?"

At this point the husband turned to the flight attendant and said, "You'll have to excuse my wife. She doesn't speak to servants."

How that must have hurt! I doubt if that flight attendant skipped to the bulkhead where her colleagues were and joyfully proclaimed, "Someone has finally recognized my true identity!" Quite the contrary. My guess is that she was deeply offended.

In contrast, the person who is awestruck by God's magnificence and has a redemptively redirected sense of significance will think, *I'll serve others on His behalf.*

Those who have high positions may feel exempt from the call to serve. Bosses, professionals, and even parents may find it hard to perceive themselves as servants. But position, whether in business, at home, or in the church, does not exempt us from exercising Christlike servanthood. Christ Himself held the highest position in the universe, and yet He used that position as a platform from which to serve! Our positions in life are but platforms to be used for servanthood.

AN ELEVATOR CLEANING

At MBI, we have a set of elevators with stainless steel doors that quickly accumulate hand and fingerprints. Our housekeeping staff does a great job of keeping the doors clean. One day, I got on the elevator and noticed one of our housekeeping staff members tackling the task. The problem was, she was so short she couldn't reach the top part of the doors. I could have thought to myself, *Isn't it a pity that someone else didn't get on to help her? Certainly the president of Moody Bible Institute is not called to a task like that.*

I knew better, of course. So I asked if I could help her reach the top of the door, and she gladly handed me the cleaning cloth. Just as I reached toward the top of the doors, the elevator stopped, the doors opened, and several of our employees got on. There I was with the cleaning equipment in my hands, busy about the task. My instinctive urge was to hand the cleaning materials back to the housekeeper quickly and look a little more "presidential" as the people entered the elevator.

But I knew that if I was to be anything like my Savior I needed to keep cleaning the doors, which I did. I had an opportunity a couple of weeks later to do the same thing. Sometime after that I was walking down the hall and saw this housekeeper. I jokingly asked her how the elevators were coming, and she beamed. "Great! In fact, lots of people are helping me with the doors now." Not only is none of us exempt from servanthood, but it's catching. And it's strategic if, through our lives, we are going to advance God's glory and the gain of His kingdom.

It's important to note the twofold focus of Christ's commitment to service. He was committed to serving His Father, and as a by-product He was a servant to people in need. Our service needs to have this same dual focus. First and foremost, we are servants of our Lord Jesus Christ. There's never a problem here because He is always worthy of our uncompromising allegiance. But when we step forward as His servants, He always sends us out to serve Him on behalf of the needs and interests of others.

Scripture is replete with references to the needs of people, and the priority of using what we have to enable, empower, and enhance the lives of others around us. But Christ's call to selfless service is incompatible with an addiction to our own significance and the flow of our misdirected energies. That's why being liberated from these is so essential.

The heart cry of the truly liberated is, "What can I do to help? How can I use my life and resources to serve you?" This is the spirit that Jesus Christ brought to earth. Because He was gladly submissive to His Father and willing to serve His Father's good pleasure, He was thrust into the arena of people with real needs—people hopelessly and helplessly bound for judgment and eternal separation from God. Christ's servanthood was focused on the glory of God and the gain of the Father's plan. Through redemption, we too are now free to *surren-*

der to His glory and gain and to *sacrifice* whatever stands in the way of effective *service* to Christ.

STEP FOUR: SUFFERING

For some of us, taking the initiative may mean a measure of *suffering*. A willingness to suffer, if necessary, is the fourth commitment in the process of becoming fully useful in advancing the Father's glory. Philippians 2:8 says of Christ, "Being found in appearance as a man, he humbled himself by becoming obedient to death—even death on a cross!" As Christ was, so we must be ready to glorify the Father and advance His cause, no matter the cost.

We have to remember that in the world we are up against a system and an adversary diametrically opposed to God's glory and kingdom. We shouldn't be surprised, then, when we encounter resistance and are called to endure a measure of suffering as we seek to advance His cause. Peter told us the same thing: "Dear friends, don't be surprised at the painful trial you are suffering, as though something strange were happening to you" (1 Peter 4:12).

The cross of Jesus Christ is the measure of suffering. His suffering was emotional, spiritual, physical, mental, and social. The cross was at the same time the most magnificent moment of God's glory and gain, and the deepest reflection of Christ's commitment to surrender, sacrifice, servanthood, and suffering. So we can be sure that when we are bent on magnifying and serving Christ, we will know times of loneliness, rejection, misunderstanding, and perhaps physical distress. For some, following Christ may even mean death.

JIM ELLIOT'S LEGACY

In the autumn of 1993 two missionary pilots, graduates of our Moody Aviation program, flew Martie and me into the jungles of Ecuador. We touched down onto a primitive airstrip in an Ecuadorian village inhabited by Auca Indians—the same Aucas who had killed Jim Elliot and his four missionary companions in 1956 (as described in chapter 3).

As the plane landed, the villagers ran to meet us. Many of these jungle people now proclaim and worship Christ as their personal Savior and welcome the planes that bring God's messengers. I was thrilled to know that because people like Jim Elliot were committed to surrender, sacrifice, service, and suffering on Christ's behalf, many of these nomads of the rain forest had received Christ as their personal Savior. What a great witness to the glory of God's redemptive power.

Our pilots and two of the villagers took us down a jungle path to a dugout canoe. We rowed five minutes down that river and stood on the beach where Elliot, Nate Saint, Roger Youderin, Pete Fleming, and Ed McCully had waited, made contact with three Aucas, and then were slaughtered by Auca warriors. The warriors had never heard the good news of Jesus Christ and thought the missionaries were evil spirits.

The bodies of the five men, pierced by spears, lay in the river for five days before a search party found them. If that's all there was to the story, we would say that their suffering was a waste, and that the suffering inflicted on their wives and children was unnecessary and unfair.

But other committed servants of Christ like Rachel Saint, Nate's sister, and Elisabeth Elliot, Jim's wife, refused to be broken by suffering. They went back to the Aucas with the love and gospel of Christ, and saw many come to Christ. Hundreds, perhaps thousands, of other young men and women gave their lives to missionary service in answer to the challenge to take the place of the martyred missionaries.

Because of all that, I was there almost forty years later in a dugout canoe with my Auca brothers in Christ. In fact, in the back of the canoe was an old man with gaping earlobes who had been a member of the killing party. Now he is a committed believer! God never wastes the suffering of those who are surrendered to Him, willing to sacrifice as His servants, to glorify Him and advance His cause.

I was very much aware that almost four decades ago, five missionaries had paid the ultimate price there to follow Christ. This, then, is the requisite commitment for those who would be liberated from the significance obsession by the indwelling Christ—those who would change the destructive energies of pleasure, pride, and passion into positive spiritual forces.

Interestingly, people wanting to become significant are reluctant to surrender, sacrifice, serve, and suffer. As significance seekers, they want people to surrender to them and their own agendas, even to sacrifice for them. They want their lives packaged with comforts, and they avoid hardship at all costs. But for those of us who have had our significance secured in Christ, we are free to follow His pattern.

Notice that Philippians 2:6–8 closes with a reference to the cross where Christ suffered so deeply. The cross is where we are restored to the source of significance: our God and our King. The cross is what makes it unnecessary for us to seek significance in the world around us. The cross enables us to be freed from a significance that competes with Christ, and it's the cross that brings us to a place where, fully satisfied in Him, we are willing to commit to His glory and gain. Because of the cross, we no longer need to violate God's boundaries to gain a sense of significance.

It is the cross that finishes the work started so long ago in the Garden of Eden, when God stripped Adam and Eve of the fig leaves they had used to cover their shame and loss. He shed the blood of an animal, and by that act of love and restoration covered their shame and drew them back to Himself. That was an early picture of the day when God Himself, in the person of His Son, would be the sacrifice for sin that would clothe us in His righteousness and restore a relationship with Him unhindered by shame, loss, and regret.

It is at the cross of Jesus Christ that our search for significance ends, where our struggle to advance, maintain, defend, and enhance self is replaced by a willing surrender to God's plans for us. Because of the cross we can gladly sacrifice to serve Him—and if necessary, suffer for His sake.

KRISTA'S STORY

On a recent trip to minister in Canada, I took the last Saturday night flight out of Chicago's O'Hare Airport to Toronto. As I boarded the jumbo jet, I noticed a young woman who had been preboarded and assigned a window seat on the far side of the plane. Her face was buried in her hands, and she was crying and clearly distraught. As I glanced at my boarding pass, I couldn't believe I was sitting right next to her. I had a briefcase full of work to do so I would be ready for my time in Canada, and I had counted on using the hour-and-thirty-five-minute flight to get it done.

As I was putting my things in the overhead bin, I thought to myself, *If the plane's not full, I'll find another seat.* My agenda was to get my work done. It would not only be inconvenient to have to deal with this distraught young woman, but I would appear far more significant in the eyes of my fellow passengers if I were busy with the work in my briefcase.

But then the Holy Spirit began to probe my self-centered attitude. I found myself wondering what Christ would do at a time like this, and I knew immediately. He would not only sit there, but He would *want* to sit there. I knew that if I were truly committed to magnifying Christ and advancing His cause, I would need to sit there and focus on her needs. It would mean surrendering to an agenda beyond myself, sacrificing my plans and perhaps the perception of others around me, serving Christ and serving her, and suffering the loss of valuable work time and the unknown of what might happen.

So I sat down. She looked up at me with tears running down her cheeks and blurted out, "I miss my daddy! I miss my daddy so much!" It was immediately obvious that this young woman, probably in her late twenties, was mentally disabled. I knew it was going to be a very long trip. As other passengers took their seats around us, she talked loudly about her fears of flying at night and other distressing emotions she was feeling.

I lowered the window blinds next to her to help calm her fears of night flying, but she continued to cry and talk loudly. She was so disruptive that before the plane took off, the man seated directly behind me asked the flight attendant if he could be moved. She moved him to the other side of the plane. As we headed for Toronto, she kept me busy changing her watch to Toronto time, answering her questions, looking at the picture book on her lap, and trying to calm her fears as she yelled at her invisible friend, "Be quiet, Michelle. I've told you to be quiet."

When they brought soft drinks and peanuts, she complained to the flight attendant about not getting a sandwich—which I thought was pretty rational considering how much I had paid for my ticket! I was completely preoccupied with helping and ministering to her. Meanwhile, the other passengers were busy with their *New York Times*, their work, or relaxing. Their occasional glances our way showed curious distance or disdain. The only recognition I received came about halfway to Toronto, when the flight attendant knelt next to me in the aisle and asked, "Sir, could I get you a free drink?"

I had learned that my fellow passenger's name was Krista, so at one point I asked her, "Krista, where are you from?"

"Wisconsin."

"Where in Wisconsin?"

"Union Grove"—which I happened to know is the location of Shepherds, one of the finest Christian homes for mentally disabled adults in America. So I asked her, "Krista, are you from Shepherds?"

"Yes, I'm from Shepherds, and tomorrow when I get home to Toronto my daddy will take me to People's Church" (one of the leading evangelical churches in that city).

I couldn't believe it. This precious lamb was from a Christian home, and God had given me the privilege of serving her. I thought to myself, "This is what angels do." No, I'm not an angel, but had all of the angelic hosts been busy that day, God might have said, "Stowell, your assignment is to sit there and help us get Krista safely from Chicago to Toronto." Suddenly, what had been a chore became a privilege, and I was struck with the fact that God had sovereignly put me there to surrender, sacrifice, and serve for His glory in her precious life.

That would have been enough to make my heart glad: to know that at least in that situation, I had been free enough of my significance obsession to yield to our Lord. But the best was yet to come.

As I stood at the baggage claim area in Toronto, the man who asked to be moved was standing next to me. "Excuse me," he said, "could I ask you a question?"

"Of course."

"Did you know that lady you were sitting next to?" I said I had never met her before. He replied, "You're kidding! Are you a therapist?"

"No, I'm not a therapist." Then I asked him what he did. He told me he was an attorney from Chicago, and we chatted briefly about that. Then he asked, "Are you a psychologist?"

I said, "No, I'm not a psychologist."

Apparently he had run out of guesses, because he asked, "Well, what do you do?"

I guess I could have said, "Having been liberated through the finished work of Christ and fully restored to the only source of significance, and no longer needing to focus my pleasure, pride, and passions on myself, I am a surrendered, sacrificing servant of God. And, if necessary, I'm willing to suffer to magnify Christ and advance His significant cause."

Needless to say, I didn't say that. Instead, I replied simply, "I'm a minister." And, as you know, all of us are really ministers of Christ.

He looked at me and said, "I knew you had to have something different in your life to do what you did on that plane." Then the bags came, and he was gone.

I pray for that attorney. I pray that he will keep running into kingdom people and noticing the difference in those who claim the name of Christ. I pray that He will come to know the liberating power of Christ for himself. And if I see that attorney in heaven, I will know that God was pleased to make me a part of His eternal work, a cause far more important than any pursuit of my own significance. In fact, to see him in heaven would indeed be significant.

> *Then I looked and heard the voice of many angels, numbering thousands upon thousands, and ten thousand times ten thousand. They encircled the throne and the living creatures and the elders. In a loud voice they sang: "Worthy is the Lamb, who was slain, to receive power and wealth and wisdom and strength and honor and glory and praise!"*
>
> *Then I heard every creature in heaven and on earth and under the earth and on the sea, and all that is in them, singing: "To him who sits on the throne and to the Lamb be praise and honor and glory and power, for ever and ever!"*
>
> *The four living creatures said, "Amen," and the elders fell down and worshiped.*
>
> *Revelation 5:11–14*

EPILOGUE

As you read this call to magnify *His* significance, you may have one nagging thought: *OK! But what about me?* When you launch your life from the platform of a significance secured in Christ into the arena of surrendering to His glory and gain, you probably will confront questions about how or when *your* needs will be met. *What about my need to relax, enjoy, to be alone, to have a friend, to be loved, understood, accepted, and affirmed?*

Good question, and I have a comforting answer. Become an "outward bound person." Outward bound people focus on Christ and on others for His glory and gain. Outward bound people have learned something wonderful about their own felt needs—the deepest satisfaction always comes when we live beyond the boundaries of "me." Consuming life on myself is far less gratifying than contributing productively to worthy endeavors beyond myself.

Yet the surrender, sacrifice, servanthood, and suffer-if-necessary sequence was never intended to produce a life of masochism. Christ Himself took time to relax, recover, and rekindle that He might be refreshed to reach beyond Himself with renewed strength. Paul told Timothy that God has given us all things to enjoy (1 Timothy 6:17). And God Himself rested on the seventh day and then instituted the Sabbath rest for His people. Within the boundaries of loyalty and obedience to God *all things* are intended for His glory and our pleasure.

In fact, one way we glorify God, reflecting what He is like, is to take pleasure in all things that are in the sphere of what is righteous and good. Laughter, love, and leisure in balance are all within the bounds of a surrendered life and, in fact, make us more effective in glorifying Him and advancing His cause.

When Chuck Swindoll told his congregation of his new plans in ministry, he took time to assure them he recognized the need for balance:

> Because these extra responsibilities will call for my best effort, I must stay physically fit and strong. A wholesome diet, a regular exercise program, and sufficient rest and sleep are big pieces to this puzzle. . . . Good health is always something I have enjoyed, along with a well-balanced sense of humor and enjoyable times of relaxation. I certainly do not intend to sacrifice those things on the altar of a schedule that has no room for fun. God deserves my very best energies and devotion and I intend to give Him both . . . but that certainly does not mean I will no longer have time to spend alone, relaxing and writing, time with my wife and family . . . or time on the ol' Harley! Some things are just too valuable even to think of giving up.[1]

None of us would argue that pastor and author Charles Swindoll hasn't lived a life of surrender to effectively glorify God and contribute in a stellar way to the gain of the kingdom. He does so and still rides Harley Davidson motorcycles. Similarly, the esteemed theologian J. I. Packer enjoys relaxing to the sounds of traditional jazz. J. Vernon McGee, prolific author, radio teacher, pastor, and Bible expositor of the last generation, was a consummate golfer, playing every chance he got. Today R. C. Sproul follows in his steps as a scratch linksman. Pastor Bill Hybels is an avid sailor who spends parts of his summer racing on Lake Michigan.

Oswald Chambers, perceived by most of us as a deeply spiritual man, with unusual intimacy with God and insight into His Word, was known for his rollicking sense of humor. In fact, after meeting Chambers for the first time, one serious young man said, "I was shocked at what I then considered his undue levity. He was the most irreverent Reverend I had ever met."[2] Chambers often took holidays in the beautiful dales and moors of North Yorkshire in England to fish its clear streams.

All of this to say that godly surrendered individuals have felt with J. I. Packer that "the Christian mission on earth is not unrelieved heroic misery."[3] Yet they have been wholly committed to God's glory and gain and have faithfully applied themselves to the task, often in sacrificial ways, as servants of the King.

There are, however, some special ones of us whom God calls for a season to sacrifice in large measure, even to suffer severely for His gain and glory. There are seasons when laughter, love, and leisure seem to elude us; when the weight and pain of God's plan to glorify Himself through us eliminates even the thought of rest or pleasure. Be assured, though, that these are seasons of great glory and gain for God. He never wastes the sacrifice and suffering of His saints. His divinely ordained deep waters are always on purpose and with purpose.

As I write this I have just finished helping Martie put up the Christmas tree and hang the garlands. In this season my mind makes its way to Mary, that teenage girl who was called on by God to surrender to an agenda far beyond herself—an agenda by which God would glorify Himself through the Savior and advance His kingdom through His Son. Her role would mean sacrifice, servanthood, and suffering.

For a moment think of Mary when the angel announced she, an unmarried woman, would carry a child. Think of the hopes and dreams for her soon-to-be marriage to Joseph that were suddenly shattered and drastically rearranged. How would she tell her parents? What would her friends and family think? Think of a barnyard birth with only lowly shepherds to celebrate. Later, a death warrant would be placed on her child's head by the fierce ruler Herod. Her son would be criticized, rejected, and ultimately sentenced to die on a cross.[4]

And though much was unknown to her, she surrendered and replied humbly to God, "Behold the bondslave of the Lord; be it done to me according to your word." And God was pleased to take her as a vessel for His glory and gain. Her season of suffering lasted more than thirty-three years before she fully realized the promises that the angels had made to her. And now she stands exalted among women as a cutting edge example to all of us of what God can do with a life fully committed to His cause.

While affirmation *finally* came for Mary, there must have been many times she wondered where her affirmation and encouragement would ever come from as she struggled with the unsettling realities of being Jesus's mother. One downside of being free to surrender to agendas beyond ourselves is that affirmation may be slow in coming. We all need affirmation, yet being liberated from our significance obsession we are no longer driven by it. Thus we need not long for or seek affirmation, having our significance secured in Him. In its purest form, significance is not something that we reach for but something that is given by God in His time and His way.

After His many hours of deep suffering on the cross, Christ found His significance given in God's way:

> Therefore God exalted him to the highest place and gave him the name that is above every name, that at the name of Jesus every knee should bow, in heaven and on earth and under the earth, and every tongue confess that Jesus Christ is Lord, to the glory of God the Father. (Philippians 2:9–11)

Although this affirmation was specifically given to Christ, we are assured, "Humble yourselves, therefore, under God's mighty hand, that *he* may exalt you in due time" (1 Peter 5:5; emphasis added).

God may affirm us through recovery from illness, times of spiritual richness, spiritual salvation for a loved one, or even professional success. Whatever or however, in time, God will provide affirmation for faithful servants. For some of us it may mean waiting for the glorious affirmation of when Christ says, "Well done, good and faithful servant" as we step across the threshold to the other side.

Whether it is in good times or tough times; whether it is a time for leisure or a time for trouble, we are commanded to "do it all for the glory of God" (1 Corinthians 10:31). Johann Sebastian Bach, who had a clear view of God's calling in life, lived, worked, and composed for the glory of God. If anyone had a right to gloat in his attainments, it was he. He came from a long line of musicians and achieved praise in his lifetime and lasting acclaim after. Yet at the end of every masterpiece he sketched the letters SDG, which stand for *Soli Deo Gloria*— "to God alone be glory."

We too will know the joy of advancing the significance of Christ and advancing His significant cause if we accept His secured significance for us as sufficient and surrender our lives to His glory and gain.

May it be said of me, of all of us, that our lives are worthy to be marked SDG, "to God alone be the glory."

> *"Now to the King eternal, immortal, invisible, the only God, be honor and glory for ever and ever. Amen."*
>
> *1 Timothy 1:17*

NOTES

CHAPTER 1: THE PURSUIT

1. R. C. Sproul, *The Hunger for Significance* (Ventura, Calif.: Regal, 1993), 21.

CHAPTER 2: PLEASURE, PRIDE, AND PASSION

1. Sam Keen, *Fire in the Belly* (New York: Bantam, 1991), 27.
2. As quoted in "Reflections," *Christianity Today*, 25 October 1993, 73.
3. Oswald Chambers, *My Utmost for His Highest* (New York: Dodd, Mead & Company, 1935), 212.

CHAPTER 3: DOWN IN MY HEART

1. Paul Johnson, *Modern Times*, (San Francisco: Harper & Row, 1991), 456.

CHAPTER 4: RANDOM LIVING

1. Lawrence J. Crabb, Jr., *Effective Biblical Counseling* (Grand Rapids: Zondervan, 1977), 61.

CHAPTER 5: THE MADNESS OF MORE

1. "Oliver" words by Lionel Bart, copyright 1960 by Lakeview Music Co. Ltd., London. Used by permission.
2. Timothy Morgan, "Sloth, Avarice, and MTV." *Christianity Today*, 4 October 1993, 14.
3. R. C. Sproul, *The Hunger for Significance* (Ventura, Calif.: Regal, 1993), 14.
4. Francis Thompson, *Thompson's Complete Poetical Works* (New York: Modern Library, 1919).
5. Chorus of "Satisfied," words by Clara Task Williams, public domain.

CHAPTER 6: SIGNIFICANCE SECURED

1. Lawrence Crabb, *Inside Out* (Colorado Springs: NavPress, 1988), 54.

CHAPTER 7: REDEMPTIVE RESTRUCTURING

1. "My Tribute" by Andraé Crouch. Copyright 1971 Bud John Songs, Inc. Used by permission.

CHAPTER 8: THE PLEASURE PURSUIT

1. C. S. Lewis, *Christian Behavior* (London: J. & J. Gray, 1943), 7.
2. As quoted in William Banowsky, *It's a Playboy World* (Old Tappan, N.J.: Revell, 1968), 122.
3. J. I. Packer, "Pleasure Principle," *Christianity Today,* 22 November 1993, 26.
4. Words by Thomas Obediah Chisholm. Copyright 1917 by Heidelburg Press. Public domain.

CHAPTER 10: PRIDE REVISED

1. C. S. Lewis, *A Mind Awake: An Anthology of C. S. Lewis,* Clyde S. Kilby, ed. (New York: Harvest, 1968), 115.

CHAPTER 11: PASSION IN PERSPECTIVE

1. Oswald Chambers, *God's Workmanship,* quoted in *Oswald Chambers: The Best from All His Books,* Harry Verploch, ed. (Nashville: Nelson, 1987), 233.
2. C. S. Lewis, *Mere Christianity* (New York: Macmillan, 1978), 104–5.
3. Words by Don Wyrtzen and L. E. Singer. Copyright © 1971 by Singspiration Music/ASCAP. All rights reserved. Used by permission of Benson Music Group, Inc.
4. Chambers, *God's Workmanship,* quoted in *Oswald Chambers: The Best,* 233.

EPILOGUE

1. Charles Swindoll, letter to congregation of the Evangelical Free Church of Fullerton (Calif.), 24 May 1993.
2. As quoted in David C. McCasland, "My Search for Oswald Chambers," *Christianity Today,* 4 October 1993, 34.
3. J. I. Packer, "Pleasure Principle," *Christianity Today,* 22 November 1993, 24–25.
4. The righteous Simeon prophesied the opposition to Jesus as well as Mary's heartache in Luke 2:34–35.